Some British Ballads

Arthur Rackham

SOME·BRITISH·BALLADS

ILLUSTRATED·BY
ARTHUR·RACKHAM

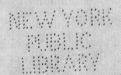
DODD·MEAD·&·Cº
NEW·YORK

CLERK COLVILL

Contents

List of Illustrations in Colour

NOTE

SEVERAL of the Ballads in this book are based on the great work of Francis James Child, *The English and Scottish Popular Ballads*, permission to use which was generously accorded by the publishers, Messrs. Houghton, Mifflin and Company, of Boston, U.S.A., to whom the grateful thanks of all concerned in the production of this book are offered.

Clerk Colvill

CLERK COLVILL and his gay ladie
 As they walked in the garden green,
  The belt about her middle jimp
Cost Clerk Colvill of crowns fifteen.

' O promise me now, Clerk Colvill,
Or it will cost ye muckle strife,
Ride never by the wells of Slane,
If ye wad live and brook your life.'

' Now speak nae mair, my gay ladie,
Now speak nae mair of that to me ;
For I ne'er saw a fair woman
I like so well as thee.'

 jimp = slim. *brook* = enjoy.

A

He's ta'en leave o' his gay lady,
Nought minding what his lady said,
And he's rode by the wells of Slane,
Where washing was a bonny maid.

'Wash on, wash on, my bonny maid,
That wash sae clean your sark of silk.'
'And weel fa' you, fair gentleman,
Your body whiter than the milk.'

He's ta'en her by the milk-white hand,
He's ta'en her by the sleeve sae green,
And he's forgotten his gay ladie,
And he's awa' with the fair maiden.

Then loud, loud cry'd the Clerk Colvill,
'O my head it pains me sair.'
'Then take, then take,' the maiden said,
'And frae my sark you'll cut a gare.'

Then she's gied him a little bane-knife,
And frae her sark he cut a share;
She's ty'd it round his whey-white face,
But ay his head it aked mair.

Then louder cry'd the Clerk Colvill,
'O sairer, sairer akes my head.'
'And sairer, sairer ever will,'
The maiden crys, 'till you be dead.'

Out then he drew his shining blade,
And thought wi' it to be her dead,
But she has vanished to a fish,
And merrily sprang into the fleed.

sark = shirt.   weel fa' = well befall.
gare = a strip.   fleed = flood.

He's mounted on his berry-broun steed,
And dowie, dowie rade he hame,
And heavily, heavily lighted doun
When to his ladie's bower he came.

'O mother, mother, lay me doun,
My gentle lady, make my bed,
O brother, take my sword and spear,
For I have seen the false mermaid.'

 *dowie* = dolefully.

The Lass of Lochroyan

'O WHA will shoe my bonny foot?
  And wha will glove my hand?
  And wha will lace my middle jimp
Wi' a lang, lang linen band?

'O wha will kame my yellow hair
With a new-made silver kame?
And wha will father my young son
Till Lord Gregory come hame?'

'Thy father will shoe thy bonny foot,
Thy mother will glove thy hand,
Thy sister will lace thy middle jimp,
Till Lord Gregory come to land.

'Thy brother will kame thy yellow hair,
With a new-made silver kame,
And God will be thy bairn's father
Till Lord Gregory come hame.'

'But I will get a bonny boat,
And I will sail the sea;
And I will gang to Lord Gregory,
Since he canna come hame to me.'

Syne she's gar'd build a bonny boat,
To sail the salt, salt sea:
The sails were o' the light green silk,
The tows o' taffety.

jimp = slender.   *kame* = comb.
gar'd = caused.   *tows* = ropes.

She hadna sailed but twenty leagues,
But twenty leagues and three,
When she met wi' a rank robber,
And a' his company.

'Now whether are ye the queen hersell,
For so ye well might be,
Or are ye the lass of Lochroyan,
Seekin' Lord Gregory?'

'O I am neither the queen,' she said,
'Nor sic I seem to be;
But I am the lass of Lochroyan,
Seekin' Lord Gregory.'

'O see na thou yon bonny bower,
It's a' covered o'er wi' tin?
When thou hast sailed it round about,
Lord Gregory is within.'

And when she saw the stately tower,
Shining sae clear and bright,
Whilk stood aboon the jawing wave,
Built on a rock of height;

Says—'Row the boat, my mariners,
And bring me to the land,
For yonder I see my love's castle
Close by the salt sea strand.'

She sailed it round, and sailed it round,
And loud, loud, cried she:
'Now break, now break, ye Fairy charms,
And set my true love free!'

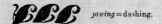

jawing = dashing.

She 's ta'en her young son in her arms,
And to the door she 's gane ;
And long she knocked, and sair she ca'd,
But answer got she nane.

'O open the door, Lord Gregory !
O open, and let me in !
For the wind blaws through my yellow hair,
And the rain drops o'er my chin.'

'Awa, awa, ye ill woman !
Ye 're no come here for good !
Ye 're but some witch, or wil' warlock,
Or mermaid o' the flood.'

'I am neither witch, nor wil' warlock,
Nor mermaid o' the sea,
But I am Annie of Lochroyan,
O open the door to me !'

'Gin thou be Annie of Lochroyan,
As I trow thou binna she,
Now tell me some o' the love tokens
That pass'd between thee and me.'

'O dinna ye mind, Lord Gregory,
As we sat at the wine,
We chang'd the rings frae our fingers,
And I can show thee thine ?

'O yours was gude, and gude enough,
But ay the best was mine ;
For yours was o' the gude red gowd,
But mine o' the diamond fine.

'Now, open the door, Lord Gregory,
Open the door, I pray!
For thy young son is in my arms,
And will be dead ere day.'

'If thou be the lass of Lochroyan
As I kenna thou be,
Tell me some mair o' the love tokens
Pass'd between me and thee.'

Fair Annie turned her round about—
'Weel! since that it be sae,
May never a woman, that has born a son,
Hae a heart sae fou o' wae!

'Take down, take down, that mast o' gowd!
Set up a mast o' tree!
It disna become a forsaken lady
To sail sae royallie.'

When the cock had crawn, and the day did dawn,
And the sun began to peep,
Then up and raise him Lord Gregory,
And sair, sair did he weep.

'Oh I hae dreamed a dream, mother,
I wish it may prove true!
That the bonny lass of Lochroyan
Was at the gate e'en now.

'O I hae dreamed a dream, mother,
The thought o't gars me greet!
That fair Annie o' Lochroyan
Lay cauld dead at my feet.'

 greet = weep.

'Gin it be for Annie of Lochroyan
That ye make a' this din,
She stood a' last night at your door,
But I trow she wanna in.'

'O wae betide ye, ill woman!
An ill death may ye die!
That wadna open the door to her,
Nor yet wad waken me.'

O he's gane down to yon shore side
As fast as he could fare;
He saw fair Annie in the boat,
But the wind it tossed her sair.

'And hey Annie! and ho Annie!
O Annie, winna ye bide.'
But ay the mair he cried Annie,
The braider grew the tide.

'And hey Annie! and ho Annie!
Dear Annie, speak to me.'
But ay the louder he cried Annie
The louder roared the sea.

The wind blew loud, the sea grew rough,
And dashed the boat on shore,
Fair Annie floated through the faem,
But the babie rose no more.

Lord Gregory tore his yellow hair,
And made a heavy moan;
Fair Annie's corpse lay at his feet,
Her bonny young son was gone.

O cherry, cherry was her cheek,
And gowden was her hair ;
But clay-cold were her rosy lips—
Nae spark o' life was there.

And first he kissed her cherry cheek,
And syne he kissed her chin,
And syne he kissed her rosy lips—
There was nae breath within.

' O wae betide my cruel mother !
An ill death may she die !
She turned my true love frae my door,
Wha came sae far to me.

' O wae betide my cruel mother !
An ill death may she die !
She turned fair Annie frae my door,
Wha died for love o' me.'

Young Bekie

YOUNG Bekie was as brave a knight
   As ever sail'd the sea;
    An' he's doen him to the court of France,
To serve for meat and fee.

He had nae been i' the court of France
   A twelvemonth nor sae long,
Till he fell in love with the king's daughter,
   An' was thrown in prison strong.

The king he had but ae daughter,
   Burd Isbel was her name;
An' she has to the prison-house gane,
   To hear the prisoner's name.

'O gin a lady wou'd borrow me,
   At her stirrup-foot I wou'd rin;
Or gin a widow wad borrow me,
   I wou'd swear to be her son.

'Or gin a virgin wou'd borrow me,
   I wou'd wed her wi' a ring;
I'd gi her ha's, I'd gie her bowers,
   The bonny towrs o' Linne.'

O barefoot, barefoot gaed she but,
   An' barefoot came she ben;
It was no for want o' hose an' shoone,
   Nor time to put them on.

borrow = ransom.   *but* = out.   *ben* = in.

YOUNG BEKIE

But a' for fear that her father dear
  Had heard her making din :
She 's stown the keys o' the prison-house door
  An' latten the prisoner gang.

O whan she saw him, Young Bekie,
  Her heart was wondrous sair !
For the mice but an' the bold rottons
  Had eaten his yallow hair.

She 's gi'en him a shaver for his beard,
  A comber till his hair,
Five hunder pound in his pocket,
  To spen', an' nae to spair.

She 's gi'en him a steed was good in need,
  An' a saddle o' royal bone,
A leash o' hounds o' ae litter,
  An' Hector called one.

Atween this twa a vow was made,
  'Twas made full solemnly,
That or three years was come an' gane,
  Well married they shou'd be.

He had nae been in 's ain country
  A twelvemonth till an end,
Till he 's forc'd to marry a duke's daughter,
  Or than lose a' his land.

' Ohon, alas ! ' says Young Bekie,
  ' I know not what to dee ;
For I canno win to Burd Isbel,
  An' she kensnae to come to me.'

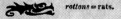 *rottons* = rats.   *royal bone* = ivory.

O it fell once upon a day
  Burd Isbel fell asleep,
An' up it starts the Billy Blind,
  An' stood at her bed-feet.

'O waken, waken, Burd Isbel,
  How can you sleep so soun',
Whan this is Bekie's wedding day,
  An' the marriage gain on ?

'Ye do ye to your mither's bowr,
  Think neither sin nor shame ;
An' ye tak twa o' your mither's marys,
  To keep ye frae thinking lang.

'Ye dress yoursel' in the red scarlet,
  An' your marys in dainty green,
An' ye pit girdles about your middles
  Wou'd buy an earldome.

'O ye gang down by yon seaside,
  An' down by yon sea-stran' ;
Sae bonny will the Hollan's boats
  Come rowin' till your han'.

'Ye set your milk-white foot abord,
  Cry, Hail ye, Domine !
An' I shal be the steerer o 't,
  To row you o'er the sea.'

She 's tane her till her mither's bowr,
  Thought neither sin nor shame,
An' she took twa o' her mither's marys,
  To keep her frae thinking lang.

Billy Blind = house goblin.
marys = maids.

O WAKEN, WAKEN, BURD ISBEL

She dressed hersel' i' the red scarlet,
  Her marys i' dainty green,
And they pat girdles about their middles
  Wou'd buy an earldome.

An' they gid down by yon sea-side,
  An' down by yon sea-stran';
Sae bonny did the Hollan' boats
  Come rowin' to their han'.

She set her milk-white foot on board,
  Cried, Hail ye, Domine!
An' the Billy Blind was the steerer o 't,
  To row her o'er the sea.

Whan she came to Young Bekie's gate,
  She heard the music play;
Sae well she kent frae a' she heard,
  It was his wedding day.

She 's pitten her han' in her pocket,
  Gi'n the porter guineas three;
'Hae, tak ye that, ye proud porter,
  Bid the bridegroom speake to me.'

O whan that he cam up the stair,
  He fell low down on his knee:
He hail'd the king, and he hail'd the queen,
  An' he hail'd him, Young Bekie.

'O I 've been porter at your gates
  This thirty years an' three;
But there 's three ladies at them now,
  Their like I never did see.

' There 's ane o' them dressd in red scarlet,
  And two in dainty green,
An' they hae girdles about their middles
  Wou'd buy an earldome.'

Then out it spake the bonny bride,
  Was a' goud to the chin :
' Gin she be braw without,' she says,
  ' We 's be as braw within.'

Then up it starts him, Young Bekie,
  An' the tears was in his e'e ;
' I 'll lay my life it 's Burd Isbel,
  Come o'er the sea to me.'

O quickly ran he down the stair,
  An' whan he saw 'twas shee,
He kindly took her in his arms,
  And kissed her tenderly.

' O hae ye forgotten, Young Bekie,
  The vow ye made to me,
Whan I took you out o' the prison strong,
  Whan ye was condemned to die ?

' I gae you a steed was good in need,
  An' a saddle o' royal bone,
A leash o' hounds o' ae litter,
  An' Hector called one.'

It was well kent what the lady said,
  That it wasnae a lee,
For at ilka word the lady spake,
  The hound fell at her knee.

'Tak hame, tak hame your daughter dear,
    A blessing gae her wi',
For I maun marry my Burd Isbel,
    That's come o'er the sea to me.'

'Is this the custom o' your house,
    Or the fashion o' your lan'.
To marry a maid in a May mornin',
    An' send her back at even?'

Chevy Chase

FYTTE I

THE Percy owt of Northombarlonde,
  an avowe to God mayd he
That he wold hunte in the mowntayns
  of Cheviot within days thre,
In the maugre of doughtè Douglas,
  and all that ever with him be.

The fattiste hartes in all Cheviot
  He wold kyll, and carry them away:
'Be my feth,' sayd the doughtè Douglas again,
  'I wyll let that hunting yf that I may.'

Then the Percy owt of Banborowe cam,
  with him a myghtee meiny,
With fifteen hondrith archers bold of blood and bone;
  they were chosen owt of shires thre.

 in the maugre of = in spite of.   *let* = hinder.
meiny = company.

This begane on a Monday at morn,
  in Cheviot the hills so hye;
The chylde may rue that ys vn-born,
  it was the mor pittè.

The drivers thorowe the woodès went,
  for to raise the deer;
Bowmen byckerte upon the bent
  with ther broad arrows cleare.

Then the wyld thorowe the woodès went,
  on every sydè shear;
Greyhoundes thorowe the grevis glent,
  for to kyll their deer.

This begane in Cheviot the hyls abune,
  yerly on a Monnyn-day;
By that it drewe to the hour off noon,
  a hondrith fat hartès ded ther lay.

They blewe a mort upon the bent,
  they 'semblede on sidès shear;
To the quarry then the Percy went,
  to see the bryttlynge of the deare.

He sayd, It was the Douglas' promise
  this day to meet me here;
But I wyste he wolde faylle, verament;
  a great oath the Percy sware.

At the laste a squire of Northomberlonde
  looked at his hand full nigh;
He was ware o' the doughtie Douglas commynge,
  with him a myghtè meiny.

byckerte = skirmished.   *wyld* = game.   *shear* = several.
grevis = groves.   *glent* = glinted, darted.
bryttlynge = cutting up.   *verament* = truly.

B

Both with spear, bylle, and brande,
  yt was a myghtee sight to see;
Hardier men, both of hart nor hande,
  were not in Cristianté.

They were twenti hondrith spear-men good,
  withoute any faile;
They were borne along by the watter o' Tweed,
  I' th' bowndes of Tividale.

'Leave off the brytlyng of the deer,' he sayd,
  'and to your bows look ye tayk good hede;
For never sithe ye were on your mothars borne
  had ye never so mickle nede.'

The doughtie Douglas on a stede,
  he rode alle his men beforne;
His armor glytter'd as did a glede;
  a bolder bairn was never born.

'Tell me whos men ye ar,' he says,
  'or whos men that ye be:
Who gave youe leave to hunte in this Cheviot chase
  in the spyt of myn and of me.'

The first man that ever him an answer mayd,
  yt was the good lord Percy:
'We wyll not tell thee whos men we ar,' he says,
  'nor whos men that we be;
But we wyll hunte here in this chase,
  in the spyt of thyne and of thee.'

glede = live coal.

'The fattist hartès in all Cheviot
  we have kyld, and cast to carry them away ':
'Be my troth,' sayd the doughtie Douglas agayn,
  'therfor one of vs shall die this day.'

Then sayd the doughtie Douglas
  unto the lord Percy :
'To kyll alle these guiltless men,
  alas, it were great pitye !

'But, Percy, thowe art a lord of lande,
  I am a yerle callyd within my contrie ;
Let all our men upon a party stande,
  and do the battell of thee and of me.'

'Nowe Crist's curse on his crowne,' sayd the lord Percy,
  ' whosoever ther-to says nay !
Be my troth, doughtie Douglas,' he says,
  ' thow shalt never see that day.

'Nethar in Ynglonde, Skottlonde, nor France,
  nor for no man of a woman born,
But, an' fortune be my chance,
  I dare meet him, one man for one.'

Then bespake a squyar of Northomberlonde,
  Richard Wytharyngton was his nam ;
'It shall never be told in Southe-Ynglonde,' he says,
  'to Kyng Harry the Fourth for sham.

'I wat youe byn great lordès twaw,
  I am a poor squyar of lande ;
I wylle never see my captayne fyght on a fielde,
  and stande my selffe and looke on,
But whylle I may my weppone wielde,
  I wylle not fayle both hart and hande.'

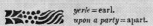 *yerle* = earl.
upon a party = apart.

That day, that day, that dredfull day!
  the first fit here I fynde;
An' youe wyll hear any more o' the huntynge o' the
      Cheviot,
  yet ys ther more behynde.

 *fit, fytts* = canto.

Chevy Chase

FYTTE II

THE Yngglyshe men hade ther bows y-bent,
  ther heartes wer good yenoughe;
The first of arrows that they shote off,
  seven skore spear-men they sloughe.

Yet bides the yerle Douglas upon the bent,
  a captayne good yenoughe,
And that was seene verament,
  for he wrought them both woe and wouche.

The Douglas partyd his host in three,
  lyk a cheif cheiften of pryde;
With sure spears of myghtie tree,
  they cum in on every syde;

Thrughe our Yngglyshe archery
  gave many a wounde fulle wyde;
Many a doughtie they garde to dy,
  which gaincd them no pryde.

sloughe = slew.   *wouche* = evil.
doughtie = doughty man.   *garde* = made.

The Ynglyshe men let ther bows be,
  and pulde owt brandes that wer brighte ;
It was a hevy syght to see
  bright swordes on basnets lyght.

Thorowe riche maile and maniple,
  many sterne they strueke down straight ;
Many a freyke that was fulle free,
  ther undar foot dyd lyght.

At last the Douglas and the Percy met,
  lyk to captayns of myght and of mayne ;
They swapte together till they both swat,
  with swordes that were of fine Milan.

These worthy freykès for to fyght,
  ther-to they were fulle fayne,
Tylle the bloode owte off their basnetes sprente,
  as euer dyd hail or rain.

'Yelde thee, Percy,' sayde the Douglas,
  'and i' feth I shalle thee brynge
Wher thowe shalte have a yerl's wages
  of Jamy our Skottish kynge.

'Thoue shalte have thy ransom free,
  I hight thee here this thinge ;
For the manfullyste man yet art thowe
  that ever I conqueryd in fielde fighttynge.'

'Nay,' sayd the Lord Percy,
  'I tolde it thee beforne,
That I wolde never yielded be
  to no man of a woman born.'

basnets = steel caps.   maniple = gauntlet.
sterne = staunch men.   freyke = bold man.
swapte = smote.   sprente = sprinkled.
hight = promise.

With that ther came an arrowe hastely,
　forthe of a myghtie wane;
It hathe strickene the yerle Douglas
　in at the brest-bane.

Thorowe liver and lungès both
　the sharpe arrowe ys gane,
That never after in all his lyffe-days
　he spayke mo words but ane:
That was, 'Fyghte ye, my merry men, whiles ye may,
　for my lyffe-days been gane.'

The Percy leaned on his brande,
　and sawe the Douglas dee;
He tooke the dede man by the hande,
　and sayd, 'Wo ys me for thee!

'To have saved thy lyffe, I wolde have partyde with
　my landes for years thre,
For a better man, of hart nor of hande,
　was not in all the north contrie.'

All that did see a Skottishe knyght,
　was callyd Sir Hugh the Montgomerye;
He saw the Douglas to the deth was dyght,
　he took a spear, a trusti tree.

He rode upon a corser
　throughe a hondrith archery:
He never stynttyde, nar never blane,
　tylle he cam to the good lord Percy.

He set upon the lorde Percy
　a dynte that was full soare;
With a sure spear of a myghtie tree
　clean thorow the body he the Percy bore,

wane = host.　　dyght = done.
blane = stayed.

O' the t'other syde that a man myght see
    a large cloth-yard and mair.
Two bettar captayns were not in Cristianté
    then that day slain were ther.

An archer of Northomberlonde
    saw slain was the lord Percy;
He bare a bende bowe in his hand,
    was made of trusti tree.

An arrow that a cloth-yarde was lang
    to the harde stele haled he;
A dynt that was both sad and soar
    he set on Sir Hugh the Montgomerye.

The dynt yt was both sad and sair
    that he on Montgomerye set;
The swane-fethars that his arrowe bare
    with his hart-blood they were wet.

Ther was never a freyke one foot wolde flee,
    but still in stour dyd stand,
Hewyng on yche othar, whylle they myghte dree
    with many a balefull brande.

This battell begane in Cheviot
    an hour befor the noon,
And when even-songe bell was rang,
    the battell was not half done.

They held their ground on ethar hande
    by the lyght of the moon;
Many hade no strength for to stande,
    in Cheviot the hills abune.

   stour = press of battle.   dree = endure.

Of fifteen hondrith archars of Ynglonde
    went away but seventi and thre ;
Of twenti hondrith spear-men of Skotlande,
    but even five and fifti.

But all were slayne Cheviot within ;
    they hade no strength to stand on hy ;
The chylde may rue that ys unborne,
    it was the more pittè.

There was slayne, with the lord Percy
    Sir John of Agerstone,
Sir Roger, the hende Hartly,
    Sir Wyllyam, the bolde Heron.

Sir Jorge, the worthè Loumley,
    a knyghte of great renowen,
Sir Ralf, the ryche Rabye,
    with dyntes were beaten dowene.

For Wetharryngton my harte was wo,
    that ever he slayne shulde be ;
For when both his leggis were hewne in two,
    yet he kneeled and fought on hys knee.

Ther was slayne, with the doughtie Douglas,
    Sir Hugh the Montgomerye,
Ser Davy Lamb, that worthè was,
    his sister's son was he.

Sir Charles a Murray in that place,
    that never a foot wolde flee ;
Sir Hugh Maxwelle, a lorde he was,
    with the Douglas dyd he dee.

 *hende* = gentle.

So on the morrowe they made them biers
   off birch and hasell so gay ;
Many widows, with wepyng tears,
   cam to fache ther makys away.

Tivydale may carpe of care,
   Northombarlond may mayk great moan,
For two such captayns as slayne were there
   On the March-parts shall neuer be non.

Word ys commen to Eddenburrowe,
   to Jamy the Skottishe kynge,
That doughtie Duglas, lyff-tenant of the Marches,
   he slain lay Chyviot within.

His handdès dyd he clasp and wryng,
   he sayd, Alas, and woe ys me !
Such an othar captayn Skotland within,
   he sayd, y-feth shuld never be.

Worde ys commyn to lovly Londone,
   till the fourth Harry our kynge,
That Lord Percy, leyff-tenante of the Marches,
   he lay slayne Cheviot within.

'God have mercy on his solle,' sayde Kyng Harry,
   'good lord, yf thy will it be !
I have a hondrith captayns in Ynglonde,' he sayd,
   'as good as ever was he :
But, Percy an' I brook my lyffe,
   thy deth well quyte shall be.'

As our noble kynge mayd his avowe,
   lyke a noble prince of renowen,
For the deth of the lord Percy
   he dyd the battell of Hombyll-down ;

makys = mates.   carpe = talk.
brook = enjoy.   quyte = quit, requited.

Wher syx and thrittè Skottishe knyghtes
  on a day wear beaten down:
Glendale glytter'd on ther armor bryght,
  over castille, towar, and town.

This was the huntynge of the Cheviot,
  that e'er begane this spurn;
Old men that knowen the grownde well yenoughe
  call it the battell of Otterburn.

At Otterburn begane this spurne,
  Upon a Monnynday;
Ther was the doughtè Doglas slain,
  the Percy never went away.

Ther was never a tym on the Marche-partès
  Since the Douglas and the Percy met,
But yt ys marvel and the rede blude ronne not,
  as the reane does in the stret.

Jesue Crist, our balys bete,
  and to the bliss vs brynge!
Thus was the huntynge of the Cheviot:
  God send vs alle good endyng!

spurn = fighting, feud (?).   *reane* = gutter.
balys = troubles.   *bete* = relieve.

The Gardener

THE gardener stands in his bower door,
  With a primrose in his hand,
  And by there came a leal maiden
As jimp's a willow wand.

'O lady, can you fancy me,
For to be my bride,
You 'll get a' the flowers in my garden,
To be to you a weed.

'The lily white shall be your smock,
Becomes your body neat;
And your head shall be deck'd with gilly-flower,
And the primrose in your breast.

'Your gown shall be o' the sweet-william,
Your coat o' camovine,
And your apron o' the salads neat,
That taste baith sweet and fine.

'Your stockings shall be o' the broad kail-blade,
That is baith broad and long;
And narrow, narrow at the coot,
And broad, broad at the brawn.

'Your gloves shall be the marygold,
All glittering to your hand,
Well spread o'er wi' the blue blaewort,
That grows in corn-land.'

jimp = slender.   weed = clothing.
coot = ankle.   brawn = calf.

THE GARDENER

'O fare you well, young man,' she says,
'Farewell, and I bid adieu,
Since you 've provided a weed for me,
Among the summer flowers,
Then I 'll provide another for you,
Among the winter showers.

'The new-fallen snow to be your smock;
Becomes your body neat;
And your head shall be deck'd with the eastern wind,
And the cold rain on your breast.

THE·GAY·GOSHAWK

'O WEEL 'S me, my gay goshawk,
    That ye can baith speak and flee;
    Ye sall carry a letter to my love,
Bring an answer back to me.'

'But how sall I your true love find,
Or how suld I her know?
I bear a tongue ne'er wi' her spake,
An eye that ne'er her saw.'

'O well sall ye my true love ken,
Sae sune as ye her see;
For, of a' the flowers of fair England,
The fairest flower is she.

'The red, that 's on my true love's cheek,
Is like blood drops on the snaw;
The white that is on her breast bare,
Like the down o' the white sea-maw.

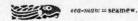 *sea-maw* = seamew.

'And even at my love's bour door,
There grows a flowering birk;
And ye maun sit and sing thereon
As she gangs to the kirk.

'And four-and-twenty fair ladyes
Will to the mass repair;
But weel may ye my ladye ken,
The fairest ladye there.'

Lord William has written a love letter,
Put it under a pinion gray;
And he is awa' to Southern land
As fast as wings can gae.

And even at that ladye's bower
There grew a flowering birk;
And he sat down and sung thereon
As she gaed to the kirk.

And weel he kent that ladye fair
Amang her maidens free;
For the flower, that springs in May morning
Was not sae sweet as she.

He lighted at the ladye's gate,
And sat him on a pin;
And sang fu' sweet the notes o' love,
Till a' was cosh within.

And first he sang a low, low note,
And syne he sang a clear;
And aye the o'erword o' the sang,
Was—'Your love can no win here.'

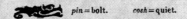 *pin* = bolt.   *cosh* = quiet.

'Feast on, feast on, my maidens a':
The wine flows you amang:
While I gang to my shot-window,
And hear yon bonny bird's sang.

'Sing on, sing on, my bonny bird,
The sang ye sung yestreen;
For weel I ken, by your sweet singing,
Ye are frae my true-love sen.'

O first he sang a merry sang,
And syne he sang a grave;
And syne he peck'd his feathers gray,
To her the letter gave.

'Have there a letter from Lord William:
He says he 's sent ye three:
He canna wait your love langer,
But for your sake he 'll die.'

'Gae bid him bake his bridal bread,
And brew his bridal ale;
And I shall meet him at Mary's kirk
Lang, lang ere it be stale.'

The lady 's gane to her chamber,
And a moanfu' woman was she,
As gin she had ta'en a sudden brash,
And were about to die.

'A boon, a boon, my father dear,
A boon I beg of thee!'
'Ask not that haughty Scottish lord,
For him you ne'er shall see.

 *brash* = sickness.

'But, for your honest asking else,
Weel granted it shall be.'
'Then gin I die in Southern land,
In Scotland bury me.

'And the first kirk that ye come to,
Ye's gar the mass be sung;
And the next kirk that ye come to,
Ye's gar the bells be rung.

'And when ye come to St. Mary's kirk,
Ye's tarry there till night.'
And so her father pledged his word,
And so his promise plight.

She has ta'en to her bigly bower,
As fast as she could fare;
And she has drunk a sleepy draught,
That she had mix'd wi' care.

And pale, pale grew her rosy cheek,
That was sae bright of blee,
And she seemed to be as surely dead
As any one could be.

Then spak her cruel step-minnie,
'Take ye the burning lead,
And drap a drap on her bosome,
To try if she be dead.'

They took a drap o' boiling lead,
They drapp'd it on her breast;
'Alas, alas!' her father cried,
'She's dead without the priest.'

gar = cause.   bigly = spacious.
blee = hue.   step-minnie = stepmother.

c

She neither chatter'd with her teeth,
Nor shiver'd with her chin;
'Alas, alas!' her father cried,
'There is nae breath within.'

Then up arose her seven brethren
And hew'd to her a bier;
They hew'd it frae the solid aik,
Laid it o'er wi' silver clear.

Then up and gat her seven sisters,
And sewed to her a kell;
And every steek that they put in,
Sewed to a siller bell.

The first Scots kirk that they cam to,
They gar'd the bells be rung,
The next Scots kirk that they cam to,
They gar'd the mass be sung.

But when they cam to St. Mary's kirk
Stude spearmen all on a raw;
And up and started Lord William,
The chieftane amang them a'.

'Set down, set down the bier,' he said,
'Let me look her upon':
But as soon as Lord William touched her hand,
Her colour began to come.

She brightened like the lily flower,
Till her pale colour was gone;
With rosy cheek, and ruby lip,
She smiled her love upon.

aik = oak.   kell = shroud.
steek = stitch.

'A morsel of your bread, my lord,
And one glass of your wine :
For I hae fasted these three lang days,
All for your sake and mine.

'Gae hame, gae hame, my seven bauld brethren!
Gae hame and blaw your horn!
I trow ye wad hae gi'en me the skaith,
But I 've gi'en you the scorn.

'Commend me to my grey father,
That wish'd my saul gude rest ;
But wae be to my cruel step dame,
Gar'd burn me on the breast.'

 *skaith* = scathe, injury.

LORD·THOMAS·AND·FAIR·ANNET

LORD THOMAS and Fair Annet
Sate a' day on a hill,
Whan night was cum, and sun was sett,
They had not talk'd their fill.

Lord Thomas said a word in jest,
Fair Annet took it ill :
'A, I will nevir wed a wife
Against my ain friends' will.'

'Gif ye wull nevir wed a wife,
A wife wull ne'ir wed yee ' :
Sae he is hame to tell his mither,
And knelt upon his knee.

'O rede, O rede, mither,' he says
'A gude rede gie to mee ;
O sall I tak the nut-browne bride,
And let Fair Annet bee ? '

'The nut-browne bride haes gowd and gear,
Fair Annet she has gat nane ;
And the little beauty Fair Annet haes,
O it wull soon be gane.'

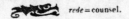 *rede* = counsel.

And he has till his brother gane,
'Now, brother, rede ye mee;
A, sall I marrie the nut-browne bride,
And let Fair Annet bee?'

'The nut-browne bride has oxen, brother,
The nut-browne bride has kye;
I wad hae ye marrie the nut-browne bride,
And cast Fair Annet bye.'

'Her oxen may dye i' the house, brother,
And her kye into the byre,
And I sall hae nothing to mysell
But a fat fadge by the fyre.'

And he has till his sister gane:
'Now, sister, rede ye mee;
O sall I marrie the nut-browne bride,
And set Fair Annet free?'

'I 'se rede ye tak Fair Annet, Thomas,
And let the browne bride alane;
Lest ye sould sigh, and say, Alace,
What is this we brought hame?'

'No, I will tak my mither's counsel,
And marrie me owt o' hand;
And I will tak the nut-browne bride,
Fair Annet may leave the land.'

Up then rose Fair Annet's father,
Twa hours or it wer day,
And he is gane into the bower
Wherein Fair Annet lay.

'Rise up, rise up, fair Annet,' he says,
'Put on your silken sheene;
Let us gae to St. Marie's kirke,
And see that rich weddeen.'

'My maides, gae to my dressing-room,
And dress to me my hair,
Whaire'ir yee laid a plait before,
See yee lay ten times mair.

'My maid, gae to my dressing-room,
And dress to me my smock;
The one half is o' holland fine,
The other o' needle-work.'

The horse Fair Annet rade upon,
He amblit like the wind;
Wi' siller he was shod before,
Wi' burning gowd behind.

Four and twenty siller bells
Wer a' tyed till his mane,
And yae tift o' the norland wind,
They tinkled ane by ane.

Four and twenty gay gude knichts
Rade by Fair Annet's side,
And four and twenty fair ladies,
As gin she had bin a bride.

And whan she cam to Marie's kirk,
She sat on Marie's stane;
The cleading that Fair Annet had on
It skinkled in their een.

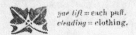
yae tift = each puff.
cleading = clothing.

And whan she cam into the kirk,
She shimmered like the sun ;
The belt that was about her waist
Was a' wi' pearles bedone.

She sat her by the nut-browne bride,
And her een they were sae clear,
Lord Thomas he clean forgat the bride,
Whan Fair Annet drew near.

He had a rose into his hand,
He gae it kisses three,
And reaching by the nut-browne bride,
Laid it on Fair Annet's knee.

Up than spak the nut-browne bride,
She spak wi' meikle spite ;
' And whair gat ye that rose-water
That does mak yee sae white ? '

The bride she drew a long bodkin
Frae out her gay head-gear,
And strake Fair Annet unto the heart,
That word spak nevir mair.

Lord Thomas he saw Fair Annet wex pale,
And marvelit what mote bee ;
But whan he saw her dear heart's blude,
A' wood-wroth waxed hee.

He drew his dagger, that was sae sharp,
That was sae sharp and meet,
And drave it into the nut-browne bride,
That fell deid at his feet.

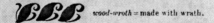 wood-wroth = made with wrath.

'Now stay for me, dear Annet,' he sed,
'Now stay, my dear,' he cry'd ;
Then strake the dagger untill his heart,
And fell deid by her side.

Lord Thomas was buried without kirk-wa',
Fair Annet within the quiere ;
And o' the tane thair grew a birk,
The other a bonny briere.

And ay they grew, and ay they threw,
As they wad faine be neare ;
And by this ye may ken right well
They were twa luvers deare.

The Twa Corbies

AS I was walking all alane,
   I heard twa corbies making a mane;
   The tane unto the tother say,
'Where sall we gang and dine to-day?'

'In behint yon auld fail dyke,
I wot there lies a new slain knight;
And nae body kens that he lies there,
But his hawk, his hound, and lady fair.

'His hound is to the hunting gane,
His hawk to fetch the wild fowl hame,
His lady's ta'en another mate,
So we may make our dinner sweet.

'Ye'll sit on his white hause bane,
And I'll pike out his bonny blue een:
Wi' ae lock o' his gowden hair,
We'll theek our nest when it grows bare.

 *corbies* = ravens.   *fail* = turf.
hause = neck.   *theek* = thatch.

'Mony a one for him makes mane,
But nane sall ken whare he is gane ;
O'er his white banes, when they are bare,
The wind sall blaw for evermair.'

Young Akin

LADY MARGARET sits in her bower door,
　　Sewing her silken seam,
　　　She heard a note in Elmond's wood,
And wish'd she there had been.

She loot the seam fa' frae her side,
And the needle to her tae,
And she is on to Elmond's wood
As fast as she cou'd gae.

She hadna pu'd a nut, a nut,
Nor broken a branch but ane,
Till by it there came Young Akin,
Says, 'Lady, lat alane.

O why pu' ye the nut, the nut,
Or why brake ye the tree?
For I am forester o' this wood:
Ye shou'd spier leave at me.'

' I 'll ask leave at no living man,
Nor yet will I at thee;
My father is king o'er a' this realm,
This wood belongs to me.'

The highest tree in Elmond's wood,
He 's pu'd it by the reet,
And he has built for her a bower,
Near by a hallow seat.

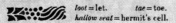

loot = let.　　　　tae = toe.　　　spier = ask.
hallow seat = hermit's cell.

He 's kept her there in Elmond's wood,
For six lang years and ane,
Till six pretty sons to him she bear,
And the seventh she 's brought home.

It fell anee upon a day,
Young Akin went from home,
And he is to the hunting gane,
Took wi' him his eldest son.

'A question I wou'd ask, father.
Gin ye woudna angry be ':
'Say on, say on, my bonny boy,
Ye 'se nae be quarrell'd by me.'

'I see my mither's cheeks aye weet,
I never can see them dry ;
And I wonder what aileth my mither,
To mourn continually.'

'Your mither was a king's daughter,
Sprung frae a high degree,
And she might hae wed some worthy prince,
Had she nae been stown by me.'

'I 'll shoot the buntin' o' the bush,
The linnet o' the tree,
And bring them to my dear mither,
See if she 'll merrier be.'

It fell upon another day,
He 's to the hunting gane,
And left his seven children to stay
Wi' their mither at hame.

 *stown = stolen.*

' O I will tell to you, mither,
Gin ye wadna angry be.'
' Speak on, speak on, my little, wee boy,
Ye 'se nae be quarrell'd by me.'

' As we came frae the hind-hunting,
We heard fine music ring.'
' My blessings on you, my bonny boy,
I wish I 'd been there my lane.'

He 's ta'en his mither by the hand,
His six brithers also,
And they are on thro' Elmond's wood,
As fast as they could go.

They wistna weel where they were gaen,
Wi' the wandering o' their feet,
They wistna weel where they were gaen,
Till at her father's gate.

' I hae nae money in my pocket,
But royal rings hae three,
I 'll gie them you, my little young son,
And ye 'll walk there for me.

' Ye 'll gie the first to the proud porter,
And he will lat you in ;
Ye 'll gie the next to the butler-boy,
And he will show you ben ;

' Ye 'll gie the third to the minstrel
That plays before the king ;
He 'll play success to the bonny boy
Came thro' the wood him lane.'

 *lane* = alone.

He gae the first to the proud porter,
And he opened an' let him in ;
He gae the next to the butler-boy,
And he has shown him ben ;

He gae the third to the minstrel
That play'd before the king ;
And he play'd success to the bonny boy
Came thro' the wood him lane.

Now when he came before the king,
Fell low down on his knee ;
The king he turned round about,
And the saut tear blinded his e'e.

' Win up, win up, my bonny boy,
Gang frae my companie ;
Ye look sae like my dear daughter,
My heart will birst in three.'

' If I look like your dear daughter,
A wonder it is none,
If I look like your dear daughter,
I am her eldest son.'

' Will ye tell me, ye little, wee boy,
Where may my Margaret be ? '
' She 's just now standing at your gates,
And my six brithers her wi'.'

' O where are all my porter-boys,
That I pay meat and fee,
To open my gates baith wide and braid ?
Let her come in to me ! '

When she came in before the king,
Fell low down on her knee;
' Win up, win up, my daughter dear,
This day ye 'll dine wi' me.'

' Ae bit I canna eat, father,
Nor ae drop can I drink,
Till I see my mither and sister dear,
For lang for them I think ! '

When she came before the queen,
Fell low down on her knee;
' Win up, win up, my daughter dear,
This day ye 'se dine wi' me.'

' Ae bit I canna eat, mither,
Nor ae drop can I drink,
Until I see my dear sister,
For lang for her I think.'

When that these two sisters met,
She hail'd her courteouslie;
' Come ben, come ben, my sister dear,
This day ye 'se dine wi' me ! '

' Ae bit I canna eat, sister,
Nor ae drop can I drink,
Until I see my dear husband,
For lang for him I think.'

' O where are all my rangers bold,
That I pay meat and fee,
To search the forest far an' wide,
And bring Akin to me ? '

 *ben* = within.

Out it speaks the little, wee boy,
' Na, na, this maunna be ;
Without ye grant a free pardon,
I hope ye 'll nae him see.'

' O here I grant a free pardon,
Well seal'd by my own han' ;
Ye may make search for Young Akin,
As soon as ever you can.'

They search'd the country wide and braid,
The forests far and near,
And found him into Elmond's wood,
Tearing his yellow hair.

' Win up, win up now, Young Akin,
Win up, and haste wi' me ;
We 're messengers come from the court,
The king wants you to see.'

' O lat him take frae me my head,
Or hang me on a tree,
For since I 've lost my dear lady,
Life 's no pleasure to me.'

' Your head will nae be touch'd, Akin,
Nor hang'd upon a tree ;
Your lady 's in her father's court,
And all he wants is thee.'

When he came in before the king,
Fell low down on his knee,
' Win up, win up, now, Young Akin,
This day ye 'se dine wi' me.'

THE TWA CORBIES

But as they were at dinner set,
The boy asked a boon :
' I wish we were in the good church,
For to get Christendoun.

' We hae lived in guid green wood,
This seven years and ane ;
But a' this time, since e'er I mind,
Was never a church within.'

' Your asking 's nae sae great, my boy,
But granted it shall be,
This day to guid church ye shall gang,
And your mither shall gang you wi'.'

When unto the guid church she came,
She at the door did stan' ;
She was sae sair sunk down wi' shame,
She coudna come farer ben.

Then out it speaks the parish priest,
And a sweet smile ga'e he :
' Come ben, come ben, my lily flower,
Present your babes to me.'

Charles, Vincent, Sam, and Dick,
And likewise John and James ;
They call'd the eldest Young Akin,
Which was his father's name.

Then they staid in the royal court,
And liv'd wi' mirth and glee,
And when her father was deceased,
Heir of the crown was she.

D

The Lament of the Border Widow

MY love he built me a bonny bower,
    And clad it a' wi' a lilye flour;
    A brawer bower ye ne'er did see.
Than my true love he built for me.

There came a man, by middle day,
He spied his sport, and went away;
And brought the king that very night,
Who brake my bower, and slew my knight.

He slew my knight, to me sae dear,
He slew my knight, and poin'd his gear;
My servants all for life did flee,
And left me in extremitie.

 *poin'd = seized.*

I sew'd his sheet, making my mane;
I watched the corpse, myself alane;
I watched his body, night and day,
No living creature came that way.

I took his body on my back,
And whiles I gaed, and whiles I satte;
I digg'd a grave, and laid him in,
And happ'd him with the sod sae green.

But think na ye my heart was sair,
When I laid the moul' on his yellow hair;
O think na ye my heart was wae,
When I turn'd about, away to gae?

Nae living man I'll love again,
Since that my lovely knight is slain;
Wi' ae lock of his yellow hair
I'll chain my heart for evermair.

Erlinton

ERLINTON had a fair daughter,
  I wat he weird her in a great sin,
  For he has built a bigly bower,
An' a' to put that lady in.

An' he has warn'd her sisters six,
An' sae has he her brethren se'en,
Outher to watch her a' the night,
Or else to seek her morn an' e'en.

She hadna been i' that bigly bower,
Na, not a night, but barely ane,
Till there was Willie, her ain true love,
Chapp'd at the door, cryin' ' Peace within !'

' O whae is this at my bower door,
That chaps sae late, or kens the gin ? '
' O it is Willie, your ain true love,
I pray you rise an' let me in !'

' But in my bower there is a wake,
An' at the wake there is a wane,
But I 'll come to the green-wood the morn,
Whar blooms the brier by mornin' dawn.'

Then she 's gane to her bed again,
Where she has layen till the cock crew thrice,
Then she said to her sisters a',
' Maidens, 'tis time for us to rise.'

 weird her in = led her into.
gin = the way of the latch.
wake . . . wane = gathering at night.

ERLINTON

She pat on her back a silken gown,
An' on her breast a siller pin,
An' she 's tane her sisters a' by the hand,
An' to the green-wood she is gane.

She hadna walk'd in the green-wood,
Na, not a mile, but barely ane,
Till there was Willie, her ain true love,
Whae frae her sisters has her ta'en.

He took her sisters by the hand,
He kiss'd them a', an' sent them hame,
An' he 's ta'en his true love him behind,
And through the green-wood they are gane.

They hadna ridden in the bonnie green-wood,
Na, not a mile, but barely ane,
When there came fifteen o' the boldest knights,
That ever bare flesh, blood, or bane.

The foremost was an aged knight,
He wore the grey hair on his chin,
Says, ' Yield to me thy lady bright,
An' thou shalt walk the woods within.'

' For me to yield my lady bright,
To such an aged knight as thee,
People wad think I war gane mad,
Or a' the courage flown frae me.'

But up then spake the second knight,
I wat he spake right boistrouslie,
' Yield me thy life, or thy lady bright,
Or here the tane of us shall die.'

 *tane* = one.

' My lady is my world's meed ;
My life I winna yield to nane ;
But if ye be men of your manhead,
Ye 'll only fight me ane by ane.'

He lighted aff his milk-white steed,
An' gae his lady him by the head,
Say'n', ' See ye dinna change your cheer,
Until ye see my body bleed.'

He set his back unto an aik,
He set his foot against a stane,
An' he has fought these fifteen men,
An' killed them a' but barely ane ;
For he has left that aged knight,
An' a' to carry the tidings hame.

When he gaed to his lady fair,
I wat he kiss'd her tenderlie ;
' Thou art mine ain love, I have thee bought ;
Now we shall walk the green-wood free.'

 meed = reward.

Babylon

THERE were three ladies lived in a bower,
    Heigho bonnie;
And they went out to pull a flower,
    On the bonnie banks o' Fordie.

They hadna pu'd a flower but ane,
    Heigho bonnie;
When up started to them a banisht man,
    On the bonnie banks o' Fordie.

He 's ta'en the first sister by the hand,
    Heigho bonnie;
And he 's turned her round and made her stand,
    On the bonnie banks o' Fordie.

' It 's whether will ye be a rank robber's wife,
    Heigho bonnie;
Or will ye die by my wee pen-knife,
    On the bonnie banks o' Fordie?'

'It 's I 'll not be a rank robber's wife,
   Heigho bonnie;
But I 'll rather die by your wee pen-knife,
   On the bonnie banks o' Fordie.'

He 's killed this may, and he 's laid her by,
   Heigho bonnie;
For to bear the red rose company,
   On the bonnie banks o' Fordie.

He 's taken the second ane by the hand,
   Heigho bonnie;
And he 's turned her round and made her stand,
   On the bonnie banks o' Fordie.

'It 's whether will ye be a rank robber's wife,
   Heigho bonnie;
Or will ye die by my wee pen-knife,
   On the bonnie banks o' Fordie?'

'I 'll not be a rank robber's wife,
   Heigho bonnie;
But I 'll rather die by your wee pen-knife,
   On the bonnie banks o' Fordie.'

He 's killed this may, and he 's laid her by,
   Heigho bonnie;
For to bear the red rose company,
   On the bonnie banks o' Fordie.

He 's taken the youngest ane by the hand,
   Heigho bonnie;
And he 's turned her round and made her stand,
   On the bonnie banks o' Fordie.

Says, 'Will ye be a rank robber's wife,
   Heigho bonnie;
Or will ye die by my wee pen-knife,
   On the bonnie banks o' Fordie?'

'I 'll not be a rank robber's wife,
   Heigho bonnie;
Nor will I die by your wee pen-knife,
   On the bonnie banks o' Fordie.

'For I hae a brother in this wood,
   Heigho bonnie;
And gin ye kill me, it 's he 'll kill thee,
   On the bonnie banks o' Fordie.'

'What 's thy brother's name? come, tell to me!'
   Heigho bonnie;
'My brother's name is Babylon,
   On the bonnie banks o' Fordie.'

'O sister, sister, what have I done,
   Heigho bonnie;
O have I done this ill to thee,
   On the bonnie banks o' Fordie.

'O since I 've done this evil deed,
   Heigho bonnie;
Good sall never be seen o' me,
   On the bonnie banks o' Fordie.'

He 's taken out his wee pen-knife,
   Heigho bonnie;
And he 's twyned himsel' o' his ain sweet life,
   On the bonnie banks o' Fordie.

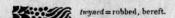 *twyned* = robbed, bereft.

May Colven

FALSE Sir John a-wooing came
　　To a maid of beauty fair;
　　May Colven was this lady's name,
Her father's only heir.

He woo'd her butt, he woo'd her ben,
He woo'd her in the ha',
Until he got this lady's consent
To mount and ride awa'.

She fetched him some of her father's gold,
And some of her mother's fee,
And he 's taken one of the best steeds
Where they stored thirty and three.

He 's got on and she 's got on,
And fast as they could flee,
Until they came to a lonesome part,
A rock by the side of the sea.

' Loup off the steed,' says false Sir John,
' Your bridal bed you see;
For I have drowned seven young ladies,
The eighth one you shall be.

' Cast off, cast off, my May Colven,
All and your silken gown,
For it 's o'er good and o'er costly
To rot in the salt sea foam.

 butt and ben = the outer and the inner room.
loup = leap.

MAY COLVEN

'Cast off, cast off, my May Colven,
All and your embroidered shoen,
For they 're o'er good and o'er costly
To rot in the salt sea foam.'

'O turn you about, O false Sir John,
And look to the leaf of the tree,
For it never became a gentleman
A naked woman to see.'

He turned himself straight round about,
To look to the leaf of the tree;
So swift as May Colven was
To throw him into the sea.

'O help, O help, my May Colven,
O help, or else I 'll drown;
I 'll take you home to your father's bower,
And set you down safe and sound.'

'No help, no help, O false Sir John,
No help, nor pity thee;
Tho' seven kings' daughters you have drowned,
But the eighth shall not be me.'

So she went on her father's steed,
As swift as she could flee,
And she came home to her father's bower
Before it was break of day.

Up then and spoke the pretty parrot:
'May Colven, where have you been?
What has become of false Sir John,
That woo'd you so late yestreen?

'He woo'd you butt, he woo'd you ben,
He woo'd you in the ha',
Until he got your own consent
For to mount and gang awa'.'

'O hold your tongue, my pretty parrot,
Lay not the blame upon me ;
Your cage shall be made o' the beaten gold
With spakes of ivorie.'

Up then spake the king himself,
In the bedchamber where he lay :
'What ails the pretty parrot,
That prattles so long ere day ? '

'There came a cat to my cage door,
And sorely frighted me,
And I was calling on May Colven
To take the cat from me.'

spakes = spindles.

Binnorie

THERE were twa sisters sat in a bour,
Binnorie, O Binnorie!
There came a knight to be their wooer,
By the bonny mill-dams o' Binnorie.

He courted the eldest with glove and ring,
Binnorie, O Binnorie!
But he lo'ed the youngest aboon a' thing,
By the bonny mill-dams o' Binnorie.

He courted the eldest with brooch and knife,
Binnorie, O Binnorie!
But he lo'ed the youngest aboon his life,
By the bonny mill-dams o' Binnorie.

The eldest she was vexed sair,
Binnorie, O Binnorie!
And sair envied her sister fair,
By the bonny mill-dams o' Binnorie.

The eldest said to the youngest ane,
Binnorie, O Binnorie!
'Will ye go and see our father's ships come in,
By the bonny mill-dams o' Binnorie?'

She's ta'en her by the lily hand,
Binnorie, O Binnorie!
And led her down to the river strand,
By the bonny mill-dams o' Binnorie.

The youngest stude upon a stane,
  Binnorie, O Binnorie!
The eldest came and pushed her in,
  By the bonny mill-dams o' Binnorie.

'O sister, sister, reach your hand,
  Binnorie, O Binnorie!
And ye shall be heir of half my land,
  By the bonny mill-dams o' Binnorie.'

'O sister, I 'll not reach my hand,
  Binnorie, O Binnorie!
And I 'll be heir of all your land,
  By the bonny mill-dams o' Binnorie.

'Shame fa' the hand that I should take,
  Binnorie, O Binnorie!
It 's twin'd me and my world's make,
  By the bonny mill-dams o' Binnorie.'

'O sister, reach me but your glove,
  Binnorie, O Binnorie!
And sweet William shall be your love,
  By the bonnie mill-dams o' Binnorie!'

'Sink on, nor hope for land or glove,
  Binnorie, O Binnorie!
And sweet William shall better be my love,
  By the bonny mill-dams o' Binnorie.'

'Your cherry cheeks and your yellow hair,
  Binnorie, O Binnorie!
Gar'd me gang maiden evermair,
  By the bonny mill-dams o' Binnorie.'

fa' = befall.   *twin'd* = divided.
make = mate.   *gar'd* = caused.

Sometimes she sunk, and sometimes she swam,
  Binnorie, O Binnorie!
Until she came to the miller's dam,
  By the bonny mill-dams o' Binnorie.

The miller's daughter was baking bread,
  Binnorie, O Binnorie!
She went for water, as she had need,
  By the bonny mill-dams o' Binnorie.

'O father, father, draw your dam,
  Binnorie, O Binnorie!
There's either a mermaid or a milk-white swan,
  By the bonny mill-dams o' Binnorie.'

The miller hasted and drew his dam,
  Binnorie, O Binnorie!
And there he found a drowned woman,
  By the bonny mill-dams o' Binnorie.

You could not see her yellow hair
  Binnorie, O Binnorie!
For gowd and pearls that were sae rare,
  By the bonny mill-dams o' Binnorie.

You could not see her middle sma',
  Binnorie, O Binnorie!
Her gowden girdle was sae bra',
  By the bonny mill-dams o' Binnorie.

A famous harper passing by,
  Binnorie, O Binnorie!
The sweet, pale face he chanced to spy,
  By the bonny mill-dams o' Binnorie.

And when he looked that ladye on,
  Binnorie, O Binnorie!
He sighed and made a heavy moan,
  By the bonny mill-dams o' Binnorie.

He made a harp of her breast bone,
  Binnorie, O Binnorie!
That he might play forever thereon,
  By the bonny mill-dams o' Binnorie.

He took three links of her yellow hair,
  Binnorie, O Binnorie!
And made it a string to his harp there,
  By the bonny mill-dams o' Binnorie.

He brought it to her father's hall,
  Binnorie, O Binnorie!
And there was the court assembled all,
  By the bonny mill-dams o' Binnorie.

He laid this harp upon a stone,
  Binnorie, O Binnorie!
And straight it began to play alone,
  By the bonny mill-dams o' Binnorie.

'O yonder sits my father, the king,
  Binnorie, O Binnorie!
And yonder sits my mother, the queen,
  By the bonny mill-dams o' Binnorie!

'And yonder stands my brother Hugh,
  Binnorie, O Binnorie!
And by him my William, sweet and true,
  By the bonny mill-dams o' Binnorie.'

But the last tune that the harp played then
  Binnorie, O Binnorie!
Was, ' Woe to my sister, false Helen! '
  By the bonny mill-dams o' Binnorie.

Get Up and Bar the Door

IT fell about the Martinmas time
   And a gay time it was then.
     When our goodwife got puddings to make,
And she's boil'd them in the pan.

The wind sae cauld blew south and north,
And blew into the floor;
Quoth our goodman to our goodwife,
'Gae out and bar the door.'

'My hand is in my hussyskap,
Goodman, as ye may see,
An' it shou'd nae be barr'd this hundred year,
It's no be barr'd for me.'

They made a paction 'tween them twa,
They made it firm and sure,
That the first word whae'er shou'd speak,
Shou'd rise and bar the door.

Then by there came two gentlemen,
At twelve o'clock at night,
And they could neither see house nor hall,
Nor coal nor candle-light.

'Now whether is this a rich man's house,
Or whether is it a poor?'
But ne'er a word was ane o' them speak,
For barring of the door.

 *hussyskap* = housewifery.

GET UP AND BAR THE DOOR

And first they ate the white puddings,
And then they ate the black,
Tho' muckle thought the goodwife to hersel',
Yet ne'er a word she spake.

Then said the one unto the other,
'Here, man, tak ye my knife;
Do ye tak aff the auld man's beard,
And I'll kiss the goodwife.'

'But there's nae water in the house,
And what shall we do than?'
'What ails ye at the pudding-broo,
That boils into the pan?'

O up then started our goodman,
An angry man was he:
'Will ye kiss my wife before my e'en,
And sca'd me wi' pudding-bree?'

Then up and started our goodwife,
Gied three skips on the floor:
'Goodman, you've spoken the foremost word,
Get up and bar the door.'

The Riddling Knight

THERE were three sisters fair and bright,
  Jennifer, Gentle, and Rosemaree,
And they three loved one valiant knight,
  As the dove flies over the mulberry tree.

The eldest sister let him in,
  Jennifer, Gentle, and Rosemaree,
And barred the door with a silver pin,
  As the dove flies over the mulberry tree.

The second sister made his bed,
  Jennifer, Gentle, and Rosemaree,
And placed soft pillows under his head,
  As the dove flies over the mulberry tree.

The youngest sister, fair and bright,
  Jennifer, Gentle, and Rosemaree,
Was resolved for to wed this valiant knight,
  As the dove flies over the mulberry tree.

'And if you can answer questions three,
  Jennifer, Gentle, and Rosemaree,
O then, fair maid, I will marry with thee,
  As the dove flies over the mulberry tree.

'O what is sharper nor a thorn?
  Jennifer, Gentle, and Rosemaree,
And what is louder nor a horn?
  As the dove flies over the mulberry tree.'

'O hunger is sharper nor a thorn,
  Jennifer, Gentle, and Rosemaree,
And shame is louder nor a horn,
  As the dove flies over the mulberry tree.'

'O what is heavier nor the lead?
  Jennifer, Gentle, and Rosemaree,
And what is better nor the bread?
  As the dove flies over the mulberry tree.'

'O sin is heavier nor the lead,
  Jennifer, Gentle, and Rosemaree,
And the blessings better nor the bread,
  As the dove flies over the mulberry tree.'

'O what is broader nor the way?
  Jennifer, Gentle, and Rosemaree,
And what is deeper nor the sea?
  As the dove flies over the mulberry tree.'

'O love is broader than the way,
  Jennifer, Gentle, and Rosemaree,
And hell is deeper than the sea,
  As the dove flies over the mulberry tree.'

' O you have answered my questions three,
  Jennifer, Gentle, and Rosemaree,
And now, fair maid, I will marry with thee,
  As the dove flies over the mulberry tree.'

Lady Elspat

'O brent 's your brow, my Lady Elspat !
   O golden yallow is your hair !
   Of all the maids of fair Scotland,
There 's nane like Lady Elspat fair.'

' Perform your vows, Sweet William,' she says,
' The vows which ye ha' made to me,
An' at the back o' my mother's castle
This night I 'll surely meet wi' thee.'

But wae be to her brother's page,
Who heard the words this twa did say !
He 's told them to her lady mother,
Who wrought Sweet William mickle wae.

For she has ta'en him, Sweet William,
An' she 's gar'd bind him wi' his bow-string,
Till the red bluide o' his fair body
Frae ilka nail o' his hand did spring.

O it fell once upon a time
That the Lord Justice came to town ;
Out has she ta'en him, Sweet William,
Brought him before the Lord Justice boun.

' An' what is the crime, now, madame,' he says,
' Has been committed by this young man ? '
' O he has broken my bonny castel
That was well biggit wi' lime an' stane.

brent = smooth.
gar'd = caused.
biggit = built.

'An' he has broken my bonny coffers,
That was well banded wi' aiken ban',
An' he has stol'n my rich jewels;
I wot he has them every one.'

Then out it spak her Lady Elspat,
As she sat by Lord Justice knee:
'Now ye has taul your tale, mother,
I pray, Lord Justice, you 'll now hear me.

'He has na broken her bonny castel,
That was well biggit wi' lime an' stane,
Nor has he stol'n her rich jewels,
For I wot she has them every one.

'But tho' he was my first true love,
An' tho' I had sworn to be his bride,
'Cause he had not a great estate,
She would this way our loves divide.'

An' out it spake the Lord Justice,
I wot the tear was in his e'e:
'I see nae fault in this young man,
Sae loose his bands, an' set him free.

'Take back your love, now, Lady Elspat,
An' my best blessing you baith upon!
For gin he be your furst true love,
He is my eldest sister's son.

'There is a steed in my stable,
Cost me baith gold and white money;
Ye 's get as mickle o' my free lan'
As he 'll ride about in a summer's day.'

   *aiken = oaken.*

JOHNNIE OF COCKERSLEE

Johnnie of Cockerslee

JOHNNIE rose up in a May morning,
   Called for water to wash his hands.
   'Gar loose to me the gude graie dogs,
That are bound wi' iron bands.'

When Johnnie's mother gat word o' that,
Her hands for dule she wrang :
' O Johnnie, for my bennison,
To the grenewood dinna gang !

' Eneugh ye hae o' the gude wheat-bread,
And eneugh o' the blude-red wine,
And therefore for nae vennison, Johnnie,
I pray ye, stir frae hame.'

But Johnnie's busk't up his gude bend bow,
His arrows, ane by ane,
And he has gane to Durrisdeer,
To hunt the dun deer down.

As he came down by Merriemass,
And in by the benty line,
There has he espied a deer lying,
Aneath a bush of ling.

Johnnie he shot, and the dun deer lap,
And he wounded her on the side,
But atween the water and the brae,
His hounds they laid her pride.

   gar = make.   *dule* = woe.
   busk't = prepared.   *lap* = leaped.

And Johnnie has bryttled the deer sae weel,
He 's had out her liver and lungs,
And wi' these he has feasted his bludey hounds
As if they had been erl's sons.

They eat sae much o' the vennison,
And drank sae much o' the blude,
That Johnnie and a' his bludey hounds
Fell asleep as they had been dead.

And by there came a silly auld carle,
An ill death mote he die!
For he 's awa to Hislinton,
Where the Seven Foresters did lie.

'What news, what news, ye gray-headed carle?
What news bring ye to me?'
'I bring nae news,' said the gray-headed carle,
'Save what these eyes did see.

'As I came down by Merriemass,
And down amang the scroggs,
The bonniest childe that ever I saw
Lay sleeping amang his dogs.

'The shirt that was upon his back
Was o' the holland fine;
The doublet which was over that
Was o' the Lincome twine.

'The buttons that were on his sleeve
Were o' the gowd sae gude;
The gude graie hounds he lay amang,
Their mouths were dyed wi' blude.

scroggs = thickets.
twine = thread.

Then out and spak the first forester,
The heid man ower them a':
'If this be Johnnie o' Breadislee,
Nae nearer will we draw.'

But up and spak the sixth forester,
His sister's son was he:
'If this be Johnnie o' Breadislee,
We soon shall gar him die.'

The first flight of arrows the foresters shot
They wounded him on the knee;
And out and spak the seventh forester,
'The next will gar him die.'

Johnnie's set his back against an aik,
His fute against a stane,
And he has slain the Seven Foresters,
He has slain them a' but ane.

He has broke three ribs in that ane's side,
But and his collar bane;
He's laid him twa-fald ower his steed,
Bade him carry the tidings hame.

'O is there na a bonnie bird
Can sing as I can say,
Could flee away to my mother's bower
And tell to fetch Johnnie away?'

The starling flew to his mother's window-stane,
It whistled and it sang,
And aye the ower-word o' the tune
Was, Johnnie tarries lang!

 aik = oak.

They made a rod o' the hazel-bush,
Another o' the slae-thorn tree,
And mony, mony were the men
At fetching our Johnnie.

Then out and spake his auld mother,
And fast her teirs did fa':
'Ye wad nae be warn'd, my son Johnnie,
Frae the hunting to bide awa.

'Aft hae I brought to Breadislee,
The less gear and the mair;
But I ne'er brought to Breadislee
What grieved my heart sae sair.

'But wae betyde that silly auld earle,
An ill death shall he die,
For the highest tree on Merriemass
Shall be his morning's fee.'

Now Johnnie's gude bend bow is broke,
And his gude graie dogs are slain,
And his bodie lies dead in Durrisdeer,
And his hunting it is done.

THE·OLD·CLOAK

THIS winter's weather waxeth cold,
    And frost doth freese on everie hill,
    And Boreas blows his blast so bold,
That all our cattell are like to spill.
Bell, my wife, who loves no strife,
    She sayd unto me quietlie,
'Rise up, and save cow Crumbocke's life;
    Man, put thine old cloake about thee.'

He. 'O Bell, why dost thou flyte and scorne?
    Thou kenst my cloak is very thin;
It is so bare and over worne;
    A cricke he thereon cannot renn.
Then I'll noe longer borrowe nor lend.
    For once I'll new appareld bee,
To-morrow I'll to towne and spend,
    For I'll have a new cloake about mee.'

 *spill* = spoil.
flyte = scold.

She. ' Cow Crumbocke is a very good cowe,
          Shee has been alwayes true to the payle,
     Still has helpt us to butter and cheese, I trow,
          And other things she will not fayle.
     I would be loth to see her pine,
          Good husband, councell take of mee,
     It is not for us to goe so fine,
          Then take thine old cloake about thee.'

He. ' My cloake it was a very good cloake,
          Itt hath been alwayes true to the weare,
     But now it is not worth a groat,
          I have had it four and forty year.
     Sometime it was of cloth ingraine,
          'Tis now but a sigh-clout, as you may see,
     It will neither hold out wind nor raine ;
          I 'll have a new cloake about me.'

She. ' It is four and fortye yeeres agoe
          Since th' one of us did the other ken ;
     And we have had betwixt us twoe
          Of children either nine or ten.
     We have brought them up to women or men ;
          In the fear of God I trow they bee.
     And why wilt thou thyself misken ?
          Man, take thine old cloake about thee.'

He. ' O Bell, my wife, why dost thou floute ?
          Now is now, and then was then.
     Seeke now all the world throughout,
          Thou kenst not clowns from gentlemen.
     They are cladd in blacke, greane, yellowe, or gray
          Soe far above their own degree.
     Once in my life I 'll do as they,
          For I 'll have a new cloake about mee.'

ingraine = vermilion.
sigh-clout = a cloth to strain milk through.

She. ' King Stephen was a worthy peere,
　　His breeches cost him but a crown.
　He held them sixpence all too deere,
　　Therefore he call'd the tailor " Lowne."
　He was a wight of high renowne,
　　And thou 'se but of a low degree ;
　Itt 's pride that putts the countreye downe,
　　Then take thine old cloake about thee.'

He. ' Bell, my wife, she loves not strife,
　　Yet she will lead me if she can ;
　And oft to live a quiet life,
　　I am forced to yield, though I 'm Good-man.
　Itt 's not for a man with a woman to threape,
　　Unless he first give o'er the plea.
　Where I began, we now mun leave,
　　And take mine old cloake about mee.'

 *threap* = dispute.

Proud Lady Margaret

FAIR Margaret was a young ladye,
  An' come of high degree,
    Fair Margaret was a young ladye,
An' proud as proud could be.

Fair Margaret was a rich ladye,
The king's cousin was she,
Fair Margaret was a riche ladye,
An' vain as vain could be.

She war'd her wealth on the gay cleedin'
That comes frae yont the sea,
She spent her time frae morning till night
Adorning her fair bodye.

At night she sate in her stately ha',
Kaimin' her yellow hair,
When in there cum like a gentle knight,
An' a white scarf he did wear.

' O what 's your will wi' me, sir knight,
O what 's your will wi' me ?
You 're the likest to my ae brother
That ever I did see.

' You 're the likest to my ae brother
That ever I hae seen,
But he 's buried in Dunfermline kirk,
A month an' mair bygane.'

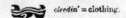 *cleedin'* = clothing.

' I 'm the likest to your ae brother
That ever ye did see,
But I canna get rest into my grave,
A' for the pride of thee.

' Leave pride, Margret, leave pride, Margret,
Leave pride an' vanity,
Ere ye see the sights that I hae seen,
Sair altered ye maun be.

' O ye come in at the kirk-door
Wi' the gowd plaits in your hair ;
But wud ye see what I hae seen,
Ye maun them a' forbear.

' O ye come in at the kirk-door
Wi' the gowd prins i' your sleeve ;
But wad ye see what I hae seen,
Ye maun gie them a' their leave.

' Leave pride, Margret, leave pride, Margret,
Leave pride an' vanity,
Ere ye see the sights that I hae seen,
Sair altered ye maun be.'

He got her in her stately ha',
Kaiming her yellow hair,
He left her on her sick, sick bed,
Shedding the saut, saut tear.

 *prins* = pins.

F

Yonge Andrew

AS I was cast in my first sleepe,
　　A dreadffull draught in my mind I drew,
　　Ffor I was dreamed of a yong man,
Some men called him Yonge Andrew.

The moone shone bright, and itt cast a ffayre light,
Sayes shee, 'Welcome, my honey, my hart, and my
　　sweete!
For I have loued thee this seven long yeere,
And our chance itt was wee could never meete.'

Then he tooke her in his armes two,
And kissed her both cheeke and chin;
And twise or thrise he kissed this may
Before they tow did part in twinn.

'Good sir, remember what you said,
And goe to the church and marry mee.'
'Goe home and fett thy fathers redd gold,
And I'le goe to the church and marry thee.'

This ladye is gone to her ffather's hall,
And well she knew where his red gold lay,
And counted fforth five hundred pound,
Besides all other jewells and chaines.

And brought itt all to Yonge Andrew,
Itt was well counted vpon his knee;
Then he tooke her by the lillye white hand,
And led her up to an hill soe hye.

 *draught* = picture.

YOUNG ANDREW

Shee had upon a gowne of blacke velvett,
(A pittyffull sight after yee shall see :)
'Put off thy clothes, bonny wenche,' he sayes,
'For noe ffoote further thoust gang with mee.'

But then shee put off her gowne of velvett,
With many salt teare from her eye,
And in a kirtle of ffine breaden silke
Shee stood beffore Yonge Andrew's eye.

Sais, 'O put off thy kirtle of silke,
Ffor some and all shall goe with mee ;
And to my owne lady I must itt beare,
Who I must needs love better then thee.'

Then shee put off her kirtle of silke,
With many a salt teare still ffrom her eye ;
In a peticoate of scarlett redd
Shee stood before Yonge Andrew's eye.

Saies, 'O put off thy peticoate,
For some and all of itt shall goe with mee ;
And to my own lady I will itt beare,
Which dwells soe ffarr in a strange countrye.'

But then she put off her peticoate,
With many a salt teare still from her eye,
And in a smocke of brave white silke
Shee stood before Yonge Andrew's eye.

Saies, 'O put off thy smocke of silke,
For some and all shall goe with mee ;
Unto my owne ladye I will itt beare,
That dwells soe ffarr in a strange countrye.'

 *breaden* = braided.

Sayes, ' O remember, Yonge Andrew,
Onee of a woman you were borne ;
And for that birth that Marye bore,
I pray you let my smocke be upon ! '

' Yes, ffayre ladye, I know itt well,
Onee of a woman I was borne ;
Yet for one birth that Mary bore,
Thy smocke shall not be left upon.'

But then shee put off her head-geere ffine ;
Shee hadd billaments worth a hundred pound ;
The hayre that was upon this bonny wench's head
Covered her bodye downe to the ground.

Then he pulled forth a Scottish brand,
And held itt there in his owne right hand ;
Saies, ' Whether wilt thou dye upon my sword's point,
    ladye,
Or wilt thou goe naked home againe ? '

' Liffe is sweet, then, sir,' said shee,
' Therefore I pray you leave mee with mine ;
Before I wold dye on your sword's point,
I had rather goe naked home againe.'

' My ffather,' shee sayes, ' is a right good erle
As any remaines in his countrye ;
If ever he doe your body take,
You 'r sure to fflower a gallow tree.

' And I have seven brethren,' shee sayes,
' And they are all hardy men and bold ;
Giff ever they doe your body take
You shall never gang quicke over the mold.'

' If your ffather be a right good erle
As any remaines in his own countrye,
Tush ! he shall never my body take,
I 'le gang soe ffast over the sea.

' If you have seven brethren,' he sayes,
' If they be never soe hardy or bold,
Tush ! they shall never my body take,
I 'le gang soe ffast into the Scottish mold.'

Now this ladye is gone to her father's hall,
When every body their rest did take ;
But the Erle which was her ffather
Lay waken for his deere daughter's sake.

' But who is that,' her ffather can say,
' That soe privilye knowes the pinn ? '
' It 's Hellen, your owne deere daughter, ffather,
I pray you rise and lett me in.

' I pray you rise and lett me in.'
' Noe, by my hood,' quoth her ffather then,
' My house thoust never come within,
Without I had my red gold againe.'

' Nay, your gold is gone, ffather,' said shee,
' I pray you rise and lett me in.'
' Then naked thou came into this world,
And naked thou shalt return againe.'

' Nay ! God fforgave His death, father,' she sayes,
' And soe I hope you will doe mee ';
' Away, away, thou cursed woman,
I pray God an ill death thou may dye.'

 *pinn* = bolt.

Shee stood soe long quacking on the ground
Till her hart it burst in three ;
And then shee ffell dead downe in a swoond,
And this was the end of this bonny ladye.

I' the morning, when her ffather gott upp,
A pittyffull sight there he might see ;
His owne deere daughter was dead, without
    clothes,
The teares that trickled fast ffrom his eye.

' Alas, that I saved her not when I could,
Fye of gold, and ffye of ffee !
For I sett soe much by my red gold
That now itt hath lost both my daughter and
    mee ! '

And daughter and gold and life he lost,
For after this time he neere dought good day,
But as flowers doth fade in the frost
So he did wast and weare away.

But let us leave talking of this ladye,
And talke some more of Yonge Andrew ;
Ffor ffalse he was to this bonny ladye,
More pitty that he had not beene true.

He was not gone a mile into the wild forrest,
Or halfe a mile into the heart of Wales,
But there caught him such a great wolf
That hee must come to tell noe more tales.

But now Yonge Andrew he is dead,
But he was never buryed under the mold,
For ther as the wolfe devoured him,
There lyes all this great erle's gold.

Sir Patrick Spens

THE king sits in Dunfermline town,
   Drinking the blude-red wine,
      'O whare will I get a skeely skipper
To sail this new ship of mine?'

O up and spake an eldern knight,
Sat at the king's right knee—
'Sir Patrick Spens is the best sailor
That ever sail'd the sea.'

Our king has written a braid letter,
And seal'd it with his hand,
And sent it to Sir Patrick Spens,
Was walking on the strand.

'To Noroway, to Noroway,
To Noroway o'er the faem,
The king's daughter of Noroway,
'Tis thou maun bring her hame.'

The first word that Sir Patrick read,
Sae loud, loud laughed he,
The neist word that Sir Patrick read,
The tear blinded his e'e.

'O wha is this has done this deed,
And tauld the king o' me,
To send us out, at this time of the year,
To sail upon the sea?

 skeely = skilful.

'Be it wind, be it weet, be it hail, be it sleet,
Our ship must sail the faem,
The king's daughter of Noroway,
'Tis we must fetch her hame.'

They hoysed their sails on Monenday morn,
Wi' a' the speed they may,
They hae landed in Noroway,
Upon a Wodensday.

They hadna been a week, a week
In Noroway, but twa,
When that the lords o' Noroway
Began aloud to say—

'Ye Scottishmen spend a' our king's goud,
And a' our queenis fee!'
'Ye lie, ye lie, ye liars loud,
Fu' loud I hear ye lie!

'For I brought as much white monie,
As gane my men and me,
And I brought a half-fou o' gude red goud,
Out o'er the sea wi' me.

'Make ready, make ready, my merrymen a'!
Our gude ship sails the morn.'
'Now, ever alack, my master dear,
I fear a deadly storm!

'I saw the new moon late yestreen,
Wi' the auld moon in her arm;
And if we gang to sea, master,
I fear we'll come to harm.'

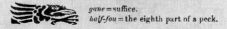

gane = suffice.
half-fou = the eighth part of a peck.

They hadna sailed a league, a league,
A league but barely three,
When the lift grew dark, and the wind blew loud,
And gurly grew the sea.

The ankers brak, and the topmasts lap,
It was sic a deadly storm ;
And the waves cam o'er the broken ship,
Till a' her sides were torn.

' O where will I get a gude sailor
To take my helm in hand,
Till I get up to the tall top-mast,
To see if I can spy land ? '

' O here am I, a sailor gude,
To take the helm in hand,
Till you go up to the tall top-mast ;
But I fear you 'll ne'er spy land.'

He hadna gane a step, a step,
A step but barely ane,
When a bolt flew out of our goodly ship,
And the salt sea came in.'

' Gae, fetch a web o' the silken claith,
Another o' the twine,
And wap them into our ship's side,
And let na the sea come in.'

They fetched a web o' the silken claith,
Another of the twine,
And they wapped them round that gude ship's side,
But still the sea came in.

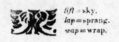

lift = sky.
lap = sprang.
wap = wrap.

O laith, laith, were our gude Scots lords
To weet their cork-heel'd shoon !
But lang or a' the play was play'd
They wat their hats aboon.

And mony was the feather bed,
That flattered on the faem,
And mony was the gude lord's son
That never mair came hame.

The ladyes wrang their fingers white,
The maidens tore their hair,
A' for the sake of their true loves;
For them they 'll see na mair.

O lang, lang may the ladyes sit,
Wi' their fans into their hand,
Before they see Sir Patrick Spens
Come sailing to the strand !

And lang, lang may the maidens sit,
Wi' their goud kaims in their hair,
A' waiting for their ain dear loves,
For them they 'll see na mair.

O forty miles off Aberdeen,
'Tis fifty fathoms deep,
And there lies gude Sir Patrick Spens,
Wi' the Scots lords at his feet.

 *flattered* = floated.
kaims = combs.

Lord Randal

'O WHERE hae ye been, Lord Randal, my son?
O where hae ye been, my handsome young man?'
'I hae been to the wild wood; mother, make
my bed soon,
For I'm weary wi' hunting, and fain wald lie down.'

'Where gat ye your dinner, Lord Randal, my son?
Where gat ye your dinner, my handsome young man?'
'I din'd wi' my true-love; mother, make my bed soon,
For I'm weary wi' hunting, and fain wald lie down.'

'What gat ye to your dinner, Lord Randal, my son?
What gat ye to your dinner, my handsome young man?'
'I gat eels boil'd in broo'; mother, make my bed soon,
For I'm weary wi' hunting, and fain wald lie down.'

'What became of your bloodhounds, Lord Randal, my
son?
What became of your bloodhounds, my handsome young
man?'
'O they swell'd and they died; mother, make my bed
soon,
For I'm weary wi' hunting, and fain wald lie down.'

'O I fear ye are poison'd, Lord Randal, my son!
O I fear ye are poison'd, my handsome young man!'
'O yes! I am poison'd! mother, make my bed soon,
For I'm sick at the heart, and I fain wald lie down.'

LORD RANDAL

THE·TWA·BROTHERS

THERE were twa brethren in the north,
  They went to the school thegither;
  The one unto the other said,
'Will you try a warsle, brither?'

They warsled up, they warsled down,
Till Sir John fell to the ground,
And there was a knife in Sir Willie's pouch,
Gi'ed him a deadly wound.

'O brither dear, take me on your back,
Carry me to yon burn clear,
And wash the blood from off my wound,
And it will bleed nae mair.'

He took him up upon his back,
Carried him to yon burn clear,
And washed the blood from off his wound,
But aye it bled the mair.

'O brither dear, take me on your back,
Carry me to yon kirk-yard,
And dig a grave baith wide and deep,
And lay my body there.'

warsle = wrestle.

He 's ta'en him up upon his back,
Carried him to yon kirk-yard,
And dug a grave baith wide and deep,
And laid his body there.

' But what will I say to my father dear,
Gin he chance to say, Willie, whar 's John ? '
' O say that he 's to England gone,
To buy him a cask of wine.'

' And what will I say to my mother dear,
Gin she chance to say, Willie, whar 's John ? '
' O say that he 's to England gone,
To buy her a new silk gown.'

' And what will I say to my sister dear,
Gin she chance to say, Willie, whar 's John ? '
' O say that he 's to England gone,
To buy her a wedding ring.'

' But what will I say to her you lo'e dear,
Gin she cry, Why tarries my John ? '
' O tell her I lie in Kirk-land fair,
And home again never will come.'

THE DUKE OF GORDON'S DAUGHTER

The Duke of Gordon's Daughter

THE Duke of Gordon has three daughters,
Elizabeth, Margaret, and Jean;
They would not stay in bonny Castle Gordon,
But they would go to bonny Aberdeen.

They had not been in Aberdeen
A twelvemonth and a day
Till Lady Jean fell in love with Captain Ogilvie,
And away with him she would gae.

Word came to the Duke of Gordon,
In the chamber where he lay,
Lady Jean has fell in love with Captain Ogilvie,
And away with him she would gae.

'Go saddle me the black horse,
And you'll ride on the grey,
And I will ride to bonny Aberdeen,
Where I have been many a day.'

They were not a mile from Aberdeen,
A mile but only three,
Till he met with his two daughters walking,
But away was Lady Jean.

'Where is your sister, maidens?
Where is your sister now?
Where is your sister, maidens,
That she is not walking with you?'

'O pardon us, honoured father,
O pardon us,' they did say;
'Lady Jean is with Captain Ogilvie,
And away with him she will gae.'

When he came to Aberdeen
And down upon the green,
There he did see Captain Ogilvie,
Training up his men.

'O wo to you, Captain Ogilvie,
And an ill death thou shalt die;
For taking to thee my daughter,
Hangèd thou shalt be.'

Duke Gordon has wrote a broad letter,
And sent it to the King,
To cause hang Captain Ogilvie,
If ever he hanged a man.

'I will not hang Captain Ogilvie,
For no lord that I see;
But I 'll cause him to put off the lace and scarlet
And put on the single livery.'

Word came to Captain Ogilvie,
In the chamber where he lay,
To cast off the gold lace and scarlet,
And put on the single livery.

'If this be for bonny Jeany Gordon,
This pennance I 'll take wi;
If this be for bonny Jeany Gordon,
All this I will dree.

 dree = endure.

Lady Jean had not been married,
Not a year but three,
Till she had a babe in every arm,
Another upon her knee.

' O but I 'm weary of wandering !
O but my fortune is bad !
It sets not the Duke of Gordon's daughter
To follow a soldier lad.

' O but I 'm weary of wandering !
O but I think lang,
It sets not the Duke of Gordon's daughter
To follow a single man.'

When they came to the Highland hills,
Cold was the frost and snow ;
Lady Jean's shoes they were all torn,
No farther could she go.

' O wo to the hills and the mountains !
Wo to the wind and the rain !
My feet is sore with going barefoot,
No farther am I able to gang.

' Wo to the hills and the mountains,
Wo to the frost and the snow,
My feet is sore with going barefoot,
No farther am I able for to go.

' O if I were at the glens of Foudlen,
Where hunting I have been,
I would find the way to bonny Castle Gordon,
Without either stockings or shoon.'

G

When she came to Castle Gordon
And down upon the green,
The porter gave out a loud shout,
'O yonder comes Lady Jean!'

'O you are welcome, bonny Jeany Gordon,
You are dear welcome to me;
You are welcome, dear Jeany Gordon,
But away with your Captain Ogilvie.'

Now over seas went the Captain,
As a soldier under command;
A message soon followed after
To come and heir his brother's land.

'Come home, you pretty Captain Ogilvie,
And heir your brother's land;
Come home, ye pretty Captain Ogilvie,
Be earl of Northumberland.'

'O what does this mean,' says the Captain,
'Where's my brother's children three?'
'They are dead and buried,
And the lands they are ready for thee.'

'Then hoist up your sails, brave Captain,
Let's be jovial and free;
I'll to Northumberland and heir my estate,
Then my dear Jeany I'll see.'

He soon came to Castle Gordon,
And down upon the green;
The porter gave out with a loud shout,
'Here comes Captain Ogilvie.'

' You 're welcome, pretty Captain Ogilvie,
Your fortune 's advanced, I hear ;
No stranger can come unto my gates,
That I do love so dear.'

' Sir, the last time I was at your gates,
You would not let me in,
I 'm come for my wife and children,
No friendship else I claim.'

' Come in, pretty Captain Ogilvie,
And drink of the beer and the wine,
And thou shalt have gold and silver
To count till the clock strike nine.'

' I 'll have none of your gold and silver,
Nor none of your white-money ;
But I 'll have bonny Jeany Gordon,
And she shall go now with me.'

Then she came tripping down the stair,
With the tear into her eye ;
One babe was at her foot,
Another upon her knee.

' You 're welcome, bonny Jeany Gordon,
With my young family ;
Mount and go to Northumberland,
There a countess thou shalt be.'

The Baron of Braikly

O INVEREY came down Deeside, whistling and
  playing,
    He 's landed at Braikly's gates at the day
    dawing.

Says, ' Baron of Braikly, are ye within ?
There 's sharp swords at the gate will gar your blood
    spin.'

The lady raise up, to the window she went,
She heard her kye lowing o'er hill and o'er bent.

' O rise up, John,' she says, ' turn back your kye,
They 're o'er the hills rinning, they 're skipping away.'

' Come to your bed, Peggie, and let the kye rin,
For were I to gang out, I would never get in.'

Then she cry'd on her women, that quickly came ben ;
' Take up your roeks, lassies, and fight a' like men.

' Though I 'm but a woman, to head you I 'll try,
Nor let these vile Highland-men steal a' our kye.'

Then up gat the baron, and cry'd for his graith,
Says, ' Lady, I 'll gang, tho' to leave you I 'm laith.

 dawing = dawning.   *graith* = harness.

'Come, kiss me, my Peggie, nor think I 'm to blame,
For I may well gang out, but I 'll never win in.'

When the Baron of Braikly rade through the close,
A gallanter baron ne'er mounted a horse.

Tho' there came wi' Inverey thirty and three,
There was nane wi' bonny Braikly but his brother
    and he.

Twa gallanter Gordons did never sword draw,
But against four and thirty, wae 's me, what was twa ?

Wi' swords and wi' daggers they did him surround,
And they 've pierc'd bonny Braikly wi' mony a wound.

Frae the head of the Dee to the banks of the Spey,
The Gordons may mourn him, and bann Inverey.

'O came ye by Braikly, and was ye in there ?
Or saw ye his Peggy dear, riving her hair ? '

'O I came by Braikly, and I was in there,
But I saw not his Peggy dear, riving her hair.'

'O fye on ye, lady, how could ye do sae ?
You open'd your gate to the faus Inverey.'

She eat wi' him, drank wi' him, welcom'd him in,
She welcom'd the villain that slew her baron.

She kept him till morning, syne bad him be gane,
And show'd him the road that he wou'd na be ta'en.

'Thro' Birss and Aboyne,' she says, 'lying in a tour,
O'er the hills of Glentanor you 'll skip in an hour.'

There is grief in the kitchen, and mirth in the ha',
But the Baron of Braikly is dead and awa'.

Up spak the son on the nourice's knee,
'Gin I live to be man, revenged I'll be.'

The Lochmaben Harper

O HEARD ye na o' the silly blind Harper,
  How lang he lived in Lochmaben town?
  And how he wad gang to fair England,
To steal the Lord Warden's Wanton Brown.

But first he gaed to his gude wyfe,
Wi' a' the haste that he could thole,
'This wark,' quo' he, 'will ne'er gae weel,
Without a mare that has a foal.'

Quo' she, 'Thou hast a gude gray mare
That can baith lance o'er laigh and hie;
Sae set thee on the gray mare's back,
And leave the foal at hame wi' me.'

So he is up to England gane,
And even as fast as he may drie;
And when he cam to Carlisle gate,
O whae was there but the Warden, he?

'Come into my hall, thou silly blind Harper,
And of thy harping let me hear!'
'O by my sooth,' quo' the silly blind Harper,
'I wad rather hae stabling for my mare.'

The Warden look'd ower his left shoulder,
And said unto his stable groom—
'Gae take the silly blind Harper's mare,
And tie her beside my Wanton Brown.'

thole = be capable of.
drie = as fast as he was able.

Then ay he harped, and ay he carped,
Till a' the lordlings footed the floor ;
But an' the music was sae sweet,
The groom hae nae mind o' the stable door.

And ay he harped, and ay he carped,
Till a' the nobles were fast asleep ;
Then quietly he took off his shoon,
And saftly down the stair did creep.

Syne to the stable door he hied,
Wi' tread as light as light could be ;
And when he opened and gaed in,
There he fand thirty steeds and three.

He took a colt's halter frae his hose,
And o' his purpose didna fail,
He slipt it ower the Wanton's nose,
And tied it to his gray mare's tail.

He turned them loose at the castle gate,
Ower muir and moss and ilka dale ;
And she ne'er let the Wanton bait,
But kept him a-galloping hame to her foal.

The mare she was right swift o' foot,
She didna fail to find the way ;
For she was at Lochmaben gate,
A lang three hours before the day.

When she cam to the harper's door,
There she gave mony a nicker and sneer ;
' Rise up,' quo' the wife, ' thou lazy lass,
Let in thy master and his mare.'

carped = sung.   sneer = snort.

Then up she rose, put on her clothes,
And keekit through at the lock-hole,
'O! by my sooth,' then cried the lass,
'Our mare has gotten a braw brown foal.'

'Come, haud thy tongue, thou silly wench,
The morn's but glancing in your e'e,'
'I 'll wad my hail fee against a groat,
He 's bigger than e'er our foal will be.'

Now all this while in merry Carlisle,
The Harper harped to hie and law,
And the fiend dought they do but listen him to,
Until that the day began to daw.

But on the morn, at fair day-light,
When they had ended a' their cheer,
Behold the Wanton Brown was gane,
And eke the poor blind Harper's mare!

'Allace, allace,' quo' the cunning auld Harper,
'And ever allace that I cam here;
In Scotland I lost a braw colt foal,
In England they 've stown my gude gray mare!'

'Come, cease thy allacing, thou silly blind Harper,
And again of thy harping let us hear,
And weel pay'd sall thy colt foal be,
And thou sall have a far better mare.'

And ay he harped, and ay he carped,
Sae swete were the harpings he let them hear,
He was paid for the foal he had never lost,
And three times ower for the gude Gray Mare.

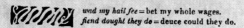 *wad my hail fee* = bet my whole wages.
fiend dought they do = deuce could they do.

The False Lover Won Back

A FAIR maid sat in her bower door
    Wringing her lily hands,
    And by it came a sprightly youth,
Fast tripping o'er the strands.

'Where gang ye, young John,' she says,
'Sae early in the day?
It gars me think, by your fast trip,
Your journey 's far away.'

He turned about wi' surly look,
And said, 'What 's that to thee?
I 'm gae'n to see a lovely maid,
Mair fairer far than ye.'

'Now hae ye play'd me this, fause love,
In simmer, 'mid the flowers?
I shall repay ye back again,
In winter, 'mid the showers.

'But again, dear love, and again, dear love,
Will ye not turn again?
For as ye look to other women,
I shall to other men.'

THE FALSE LOVER WON BACK

' Make your choice of whom you please,
For I my choice will have,
I 've chosen a maid more fair than thee,
I never will deceive.'

But she 's kilt up her claithing fine,
And after him gaed she ;
But aye he said, ' Ye 'll turn again,
Nae farther gae wi' me.'

' But again, dear love, and again, dear love,
Will ye ne'er love me again ?
Alas for loving you sae well,
And you nae me again.'

The firstan town that they came till,
He bought her brooch and ring,
And aye he bade her turn again,
And gang nae farther wi' him.

' But again, dear love, and again, dear love,
Will ye ne'er love me again ?
Alas for loving you sae well,
But you nae me again.'

The nextan town that they came till,
He bought her muff and gloves,
But aye he bade her turn again,
And choose some other loves.

' But again, dear love, and again, dear love,
Will ye ne'er love me again ?
Alas for loving you sae well,
And you nae me again.'

The nextan town that they came till,
His heart it grew mair fain,
And he was as deep in love wi' her
As she was ower again.

The nextan town that they came till,
He bought her wedding gown,
And made her lady of ha's and bowers,
Into sweet Berwick town.

Lamkin

IT 'S Lamkin was a mason good
   As ever built wi' stane ;
   He built Lord Wearie's castle,
But payment got he nane.

'O pay me, Lord Wearie,
Come, pay me my fee ' ;
'I canna pay you, Lamkin,
For I maun gang o'er the sea.'

'O pay me now, Lord Wearie,
Come, pay me out o' hand ' ;
'I canna pay you, Lamkin,
Unless I sell my land.'

'O gin ye winna pay me,
I here sall make a vow,
Before that ye come hame again,
Ye sall hae cause to rue.'

Lord Wearie got a bonny ship
To sail the saut sea faem ;
Bade his lady weel the castle keep,
Ay till he should come hame.

But the nourice was a fause limmer
As e'er hung on a tree ;
She laid a plot wi' Lamkin,
Whan her lord was o'er the sea.

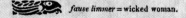 _fause limmer_ = wicked woman.

She laid a plot wi' Lamkin,
When the servants were awa,
Loot him in at a little shot-window,
And brought him to the ha'.

'O whare 's a' the men o' this house,
That ca' me Lamkin ? '
'They 're at the barn-well thrashing;
'Twill be lang ere they come in.'

'And whare 's the women o' this house,
That ca' me Lamkin ? '
'They 're at the far well washing;
'Twill be lang ere they come in.'

'And whare 's the bairns o' this house,
That ca' me Lamkin ? '
'They 're at the school reading;
'Twill be night or they come hame.'

'O whare 's the lady o' this house
That ca's me Lamkin ? '
'She 's up in her bower sewing,
But we soon can bring her down.'

Then Lamkin 's tane a sharp knife,
That hang down by his gaire,
And he has gi'en the bonny babe
A deep wound and a sair.

Then Lamkin he rocked,
And the fause nourice sang,
Till frae ilkae bore o' the cradle
The red blood out sprang.

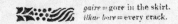

gaire = gore in the skirt.
ilkae bore = every crack.

Then out it spak the lady,
As she stood on the stair :
' What ails my bairn, nourice,
That he 's greeting sae sair.

' O still my bairn, nourice,
O still him wi' the pap ! '
' He winna still, lady,
For this nor for that.'

' O still my bairn, nourice,
O still him wi' the wand ! '
' He winna still, lady,
For a' his father's land.'

' O still my bairn, nourice,
O still him wi' the bell ! '
' He winna still, lady,
Till ye come down yoursel.'

O the firsten step she steppit,
She steppit on a stane ;
But the neisten step she steppit,
She met him Lamkin.

' O mercy, mercy, Lamkin,
Hae mercy upon me !
Though you 've ta'en my young son's life,
Ye may let mysel be.'

' O sall I kill her, nourice,
Or sall I lat her be ? '
' O kill her, kill her, Lamkin,
For she ne'er was good to me.'

 *greeting* = crying.

'O scour the bason, nourice,
And mak' it fair and clean,
For to keep this lady's heart's blood,
For she's come o' noble kin.'

'There need nae bason, Lamkin,
Lat it run through the floor;
What better is the heart's blood
O' the rich than o' the poor?'

But ere three months were at an end,
Lord Wearie came again;
But dowie, dowie was his heart
When first he came hame.

'O wha's blood is this,' he says,
'That lies in the chamer?'
'It is your lady's blood;
'Tis as clear as the lamer.'

'And wha's blood is this,' he says,
'That lies in my ha'?'
'It is your young son's heart's blood;
'Tis the clearest ava'.'

O sweetly sang the blackbird
That sat upon the tree:
But sairer grat Lamkin,
When he was condemned to die.

And bonny sang the mavis,
Out o' the thorny brake;
But sairer grat the nourice,
When she was tied to the stake.

dowie = doleful.   *chamer* = chamber.
lamer = amber.   *ava'* = of all.
grat = cried.

Bonnie George Campbell

Hie upon Hielands,
  And laigh upon Tay,
  Bonnie George Campbell
Rode out on a day.

Saddled and bridled
And gallant rode he.
Hame cam his guid horse,
But never cam he.

Out cam his mother dear,
Greeting fu' sair ;
And out cam his bonnie bryde,
Riving her hair.

' My meadow lies green,
My corn is unshorn,
My barn is to build,
And my babe is unborn.'

Saddled and bridled
And booted rode he,
A plume in his helmet,
A sword at his knee.

But toom cam his saddle,
A' bluidy to see ;
Oh, hame cam his guid horse,
But never cam he.

laigh = low.   *greeting* = crying.
toom = empty.

H

Prince Robert

PRINCE ROBERT has wedded a gay ladye,
  He has wedded her with a ring;
  Prince Robert has wedded a gay ladye,
But he darna' bring her hame.

'Your blessing, your blessing, my mother dear!
Your blessing now grant to me!'
'Instead of a blessing ye sall have my curse,
And you 'll get nae blessing frae me.'

She has called upon her waiting maid,
To fill a glass of wine;
She has called upon her fause steward,
To put rank poison in.

She has put it to her roudes lip,
And to her roudes chin;
She has put it to her fause, fause mouth,
But the never a drap gaed in.

He has put it to his bonny mouth,
And to his bonny chin,
He 's put it to his cherry lip,
And sae fast the rank poison ran in.

'O ye hae poisoned your ae son, mother.
Your ae son and your heir;
O ye hae poisoned your ae son, mother.
And sons you 'll never hae mair.'

 *roudes* = haggard.

'O where will I get a little boy
That will win hose and shoon,
To run sae fast to Darlinton,
And bid fair Eleanor come?'

Then up and spake a little boy,
That wad win hose and shoon,
'O I'll away to Darlinton,
And bid fair Eleanor come.'

O he has run to Darlinton,
And tirled at the pin;
And wha was sae ready as Eleanor's sel'
To let the bonny boy in?

'Your gude-mother has made ye a rare dinour,
She's made it baith gude and fine;
Your gude-mother has made ye a gay dinour,
And ye maun cum till her and dine.'

It's twenty lang miles to Sillertoun town,
The langest that ever were gane;
But the steed it was wight, and the lady was light,
And she cam linkin' in.

But when she cam to Sillertoun town,
And into Sillertoun ha',
The torches were burning, the ladies were mourning,
And they were weeping a'.

'O where is now my wedded lord,
And where now can he be?
O where is now my wedded lord?
For him I canna see.'

tirled = rattled.   *pin* = bolt.
wight = fleet.   *linkin'* = riding briskly.

'Your wedded lord is dead,' she says,
'And just gane to be laid in the clay;
Your wedded lord is dead,' she says,
'And just gane to be buried this day.

'Ye 'se get nane o' his gowd, ye 'se get nane o' his gear,
Ye 'se get nae thing frae me;
Ye 'se no get an inch o' his gude broad land,
Tho' your heart suld burst in three.'

'I want nane o' his gowd, I want nane o' his gear,
I want nae land frae thee;
But I 'll hae the ring that 's on his finger,
For them he did promise to me.'

'Ye 'se no get the ring that 's on his finger,
Ye 'se no get them frae me;
Ye 'se no get the ring that 's on his finger,
An' your heart suld burst in three.'

She 's turned her back unto the wa',
And her face unto a rock;
And there, before the mother's face,
Her very heart it broke.

The tane was buried in Mary's kirk,
The tother in Marie's quire,
And out o' the tane there sprang a birk,
And out o' the tother a brier.

And thae twa met, and thae twa plat,
The birk but and the brier;
And by that ye may very weel ken,
They were twa lovers dear.

EARL MAR'S DAUGHTER

Earl Mar's Daughter

IT was untill a pleasant time
    Upon a simmer's day,
    The noble Earl of Mar's daughter
Went forth to sport and play.

As thus she did amuse herself,
Below a green aik tree,
There she saw a sprightly doo
Set on a tower sae hie.

' O Coo-me-doo, my love sae true,
If ye 'll come down to me,
Ye 'se hae a cage o' guid red gowd
Instead o' simple tree.

' I 'll put gowd hingers roun' your cage,
And siller roun' your wa';
I 'll gar ye shine as fair a bird
As ony o' them a'.'

But she hadnae these words well spoke,
Nor yet these words well said,
Till Coo-me-doo flew frae the tower
And lighted on her head.

Then she has brought this pretty bird
Hame to her bowers and ha',
And made him shine as fair a bird
As ony o' them a'.

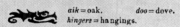 *aik* = oak.　　*doo* = dove.
hingers = hangings.

When day was gane, and night was come,
About the evening tide,
This lady spied a sprightly youth
Stand straight up by her side.

' From whence came ye, young man ? ' she said ;
' That does surprise me sair ;
My door was bolted right secure ;
What way hae ye come here ? '

' O haud your tongue, ye lady fair,
Lat a' your folly be ;
Mind ye not on your turtle-doo
Last day ye brought wi' thee ? '

' O tell me mair, young man,' she said,
' This does surprise me now ;
What country hae ye come frae ?
What pedigree are you ? '

' My mither lives on foreign isles,
She has nae mair but me ;
She is a queen o' wealth and state,
And birth and high degree.

' Likewise well skilled in magic spells,
As ye may plainly see,
And she transformed me to yon shape,
To charm such maids as thee.

' And it was but this verra day
That I came ower the sea ;
Your lovely face did me enchant,
I 'll live and dee wi' thee.'

' O Coo-me-doo, my luve sae true,
Nae mair frae me ye 'se gae ';
' That 's never my intent, my luve,
As ye said, it shall be sae.'

Then he has staid in bower wi' her
For sax lang years and ane,
Till sax young sons to him she bare,
And the seventh she 's brought hame.

But aye as ever a child was born,
He carried them away,
And brought them to his mither's care
As fast as he could fly.

Thus he has staid in bower wi' her
For seven long years and three ;
There came a lord o' high renown
To court this fair ladie.

But still his proffer she refused,
And a' his presents too ;
Says, ' I 'm content to live alane
Wi' my bird, Coo-me-doo.'

Her father sware a solemn oath
Amang the nobles all,
' The morn, or ere I eat or drink,
This bird I will gar kill.'

The bird was sitting in his cage,
And heard what they did say ;
And when he found they were dismissed,
Says, ' Wae 's me for this day.

'Before that I do langer stay,
And thus to be forlorn;
I'll gang unto my mither's bower,
Where I was bred and born.'

Then Coo-me-doo took flight and flew,
Beyond the raging sea,
And lighted near his mither's castle,
On a tower o' gowd sae hie.

As his mither was wauking out,
To see what she could see,
And there she saw her little son,
Set on the tower sae hie.

'Get the dancers here to dance,' she said,
'And minstrells for to play;
For here's my young son, Florentine,
Come here wi' me to stay.

'Get nae dancers to dance, mither,
Nor minstrells for to play,
For the mither o' my seven sons,
The morn's her wedding-day.'

'O tell me, tell me, Florentine,
Tell me, and tell me true,
Tell me this day without a flaw,
What I will do for you.'

'Instead o' dancers to dance, mither,
Or minstrells for to play,
Turn four-and-twenty wall-wight men
Like storks in feathers gray:

 *wall-wight* = strong.

'My seven sons in seven swans,
Aboon their heads to flee ;
And I mysell a gay goshawk,
A bird o' high degree.'

Then sighin' said the queen hersell,
'That thing 's too high for me ' ;
But she applied to an auld woman,
Who had mair skill than she.

Instead o' dancers to dance a dance,
Or minstrells for to play,
Four-and-twenty wall-wight men
Turn'd birds o' feathers gray ;

His seven sons in seven swans,
Aboon their heads to flee ;
And he himsell a gay goshawk,
A bird o' high degree.

This flock o' birds took flight and flew
Beyond the raging sea,
And landed near the Earl Mar's castle,
Took shelter in every tree.

They were a flock o' pretty birds,
Right comely to be seen ;
The people view'd them wi' surprise,
As they danced on the green.

These birds ascended frae the tree
And lighted on the ha',
And at the last wi' force did flee
Amang the nobles a'.

The storks there seized some o' the men,
They could neither fight nor flee;
The swans they bound the bride's best man
Below a green aik tree.

They lighted next on maidens fair,
Then on the bride's own head,
And wi' the twinkling o' an e'e,
The bride and them were fled.

There 's ancient men at weddings been
For sixty years or more;
But sic a curious wedding-day
They never saw before.

For naething cou'd the companie do,
Nor naething cou'd they say;
But they saw a flock o' pretty birds
That took their bride away.

THE·DEATH·OF·PARCY·REED

GOD send the land deliverance
 Frae every reaving, riding Scot;
  We 'll sune hae neither cow nor ewe,
We 'll sune hae neither staig nor stot.

The outlaws come frae Liddesdale,
They herry Redesdale far and near;
The rich man's gelding it maun gang,
They canna pass the puir man's mare.

Sure it were weel, had ilka thief,
Around his neck a halter strang;
And curses heavy may they light
On traitors vile oursels amang.

Now Parcy Reed has Crosier ta'en,
He has delivered him to the law;
But Crosier says he 'll do waur than that,
He 'll make the tower o' Troughend fa'.

And Crosier says he will do waur,
He will do waur if waur can be,
He 'll make the bairns a' fatherless,
And then, the land it may lie lee.

' To the hunting, ho ! ' cried Parcy Reed,
' The morning sun is on the dew ;
The cauler breeze frae off the fells,
Will lead the dogs to the quarry true.

' To the hunting, ho ! ' cried Parcy Reed,
And to the hunting he has gane ;
And the three fause Ha's o' Girsonsfield
Alang wi' him he has them ta'en.

They hunted high, they hunted low,
By heathery hill and birken shaw ;
They raised a buck on Rooken Edge,
And blew the mort at fair Ealylawe.

They hunted high, they hunted low,
They made the echoes ring amain ;
With music sweet o' horn and hound,
They merry made fair Redesdale glen.

They hunted high, they hunted low,
They hunted up, they hunted down,
Until the day was past the prime,
And it grew late in the afternoon.

They hunted high in Batinghope,
When as the sun was sinking low,
Says Parcy then, ' Ca' off the dogs,
We 'll bait our steeds and homeward go.'

They lighted high in Batinghope,
Atween the brown and benty ground;
They had but rested a little while
Till Parcy Reed was sleeping sound.

There 's nane may lean on a rotten staff,
But him that risks to get a fa';
There 's nane may in a traitor trust,
And traitors black were every Ha'.

They 've stown the bridle off his steed,
And they 've put water in his lang gun;
They 've fixed his sword within the sheath
That out again it winna come.

' Awaken ye, awaken ye, Parcy Reed,
Or by your enemies be ta'en,
For yonder are the five Crosiers
A-coming owre the Hingin-stane.'

' If they be five, and we be four,
Sae that ye stand alang wi' me,
Then every man ye will tak one,
And only leave but two to me:
We will then meet as brave men ought,
And make them either fight or flee.'

' We mayna stand, we canna stand,
We daurna stand alang wi' thee;
The Crosiers haud thee at a feud,
And they wad kill baith thee and we.'

' O turn thee, turn thee, Johnie Ha',
O turn thee, man, and fight wi' me;
When ye come to Troughend again,
My gude black naig I will gi'e thee;
He cost full twenty pound o' gowd,
Atween my brother John and me.'

'I mayna turn, I canna turn,
I daurna turn and fight wi' thee ;
The Crosiers haud thee at a feud,
And they wad kill baith thee and me.'

'O turn thee, turn thee, Willie Ha',
O turn thee, man, and fight wi' me :
When ye come to Troughend again,
A yoke o' owsen I 'll gi'e thee.'

'I mayna turn, I canna turn,
I daurna turn and fight wi' thee ;
The Crosiers haud thee at a feud,
And they wad kill baith thee and me.'

'O turn thee, turn thee, Tommy Ha',
O turn now, man, and fight wi' me :
If ever we come to Troughend again,
My daughter Jean I 'll gi'e to thee.'

'I mayna turn, I canna turn,
I daurna turn and fight wi' thee ;
The Crosiers haud thee at a feud,
And they wad kill baith thee and me.'

'O shame upon ye, traitors a' !
I wish your hames ye may never see ;
Ye 've stown the bridle off my naig,
And I can neither fight nor flee.

'Ye 've stown the bridle off my naig,
And ye 've put water i' my lang gun,
Ye 've fixed my sword within the sheath,
That out again it winna come.'

He had but time to cross himsel',
A prayer he hadna time to say,
Till round him came the Crosiers keen,
All riding graithed and in array.

'Weel met, weel met, now, Parcy Reed,
Thou art the very man we sought,
Owre lang hae we been in your debt,
Now will we pay you as we ought.

'We'll pay thee at the nearest tree,
Where we shall hang thee like a hound.'
Brave Parcy rais'd his fankit sword,
And fell'd the foremost to the ground.

Alake, and wae for Parcy Reed,
Alake, he was an unarmed man,
Four weapons pierced him all at once,
As they assailed him there and than.

They fell upon him all at once,
They mangled him most cruellie,
The slightest wound might caused his deid,
And they hae gi'en him thirty-three;
They hacked off his hands and feet,
And left him lying on the lee.

'Now Parcy Reed, we've paid our debt,
Ye canna weel dispute the tale,'
The Crosiers said, and off they rade;
They rade the airt o' Liddesdale.

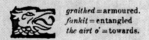

graithed = armoured.
fankit = entangled
the airt o' = towards.

It was the hour o' gloaming gray,
When herds come in frae fauld and pen;
A herd he saw a huntsman lie,
Says he, 'Can this be Laird Troughen' ? '

'There 's some will ca' me Parcy Reed,
And some will ca' me Laird Troughen',
It 's little matter what they ca' me,
My faes hae made me ill to ken.

'There 's some will ca' me Parcy Reed,
And speak my praise in tower and town;
It 's little matter what they do now,
My life-blood rudds the heather down.

'There 's some will ca' me Parcy Reed,
And a' my virtues say and sing,
I would much rather have just now
A draught o' water frae the spring.'

The herd flung aff his clouted shoon
And to the nearest fountain ran,
He made his bonnet serve a cup,
And wan the blessing o' the dying man.

'Now, honest herd, ye maun do mair,
Ye maun do mair, as I you tell,
Ye maun bear tidings to Troughend,
And bear likewise my last farewell.

'A farewell to my wedded wife,
A farewell to my brother John,
Wha sits into the Troughend tower
Wi' heart as black as any stone.

'A farewell to my daughter Jean.
A farewell to my young sons five,
Had they been at their father's hand,
I had this night been man alive.

'A farewell to my followers a',
And a' my neighbours gude at need,
Bid them think how the treacherous Ha's
Betrayed the life o' Parcy Reed.

'The laird o' Clennel bears my bow,
The laird o' Brandon bears my brand,
Whene'er they ride i' the Border-side,
They 'll mind the fate o' the laird Troughend.'

I

Hynd Horn

'HYND HORN fair, and Hynd Horn free,
  With a hey lillelu and a ho lo lan ;
    O where were you born, in what countrie?'
With a hey down and a hey diddle downie.

'In gude greenwood, there I was born,
  With a hey lillelu and a ho lo lan ;
And all my forbears me beforn.
  With a hey down and a hey diddle downie.

'O seven years I served the king,
  With a hey lillelu and a ho lo lan ;
And as for wages, I never gat nane ;
  With a hey down and a hey diddle downie.

'But ae sight o' his ae daughter,
  With a hey lillelu and a ho lo lan ;
And that was thro' an augre bore.'
  With a hey down and a hey diddle downie.

The king an angry man was he ;
  With a hey lillelu and a ho lo lan ;
He sent young Hynd Horn to the sea.
  With a hey down and a hey diddle downie.

He 's gien to her a silver wand,
  With a hey lillelu and a ho lo lan ;
With seven living laverocks sitting thereon.
  With a hey down and a hey diddle downie.

 *laverocks = larks.*

HYND HORN

She 's gien to him a diamond ring,
  With a hey lillelu and a ho lo lan ;
With seven bright diamonds set therein.
  With a hey down and a hey diddle downie.

' As lang 's this ring it keeps the hue,
  With a hey lillelu and a ho lo lan ;
Ye 'll know I am a lover true :
  With a hey down and a hey diddle downie.

' But when the ring turns pale and wan,
  With a hey lillelu and a ho lo lan ;
Ye 'll know I love another man.'
  With a hey down and a hey diddle downie.

He hoist up sails, and awa' sail'd he,
  With a hey lillelu and a ho lo lan ;
And sail'd into a far countrie.
  With a hey down and a hey diddle downie.

One day he look'd his ring upon,
  With a hey lillelu and a ho lo lan ;
He knew she loved another man.
  With a hey down and a hey diddle downie.

He hoist up sails and home came he,
  With a hey lillelu and a ho lo lan ;
Home unto his ain countrie.
  With a hey down and a hey diddle downie.

He left the sea and came to land,
  With a hey lillelu and a ho lo lan ;
And the first that he met was an auld beggar man.
  With a hey down and a hey diddle downie.

'What news, what news, my gude auld man?
  With a hey lillelu and a ho lo lan;
What news, what news, by sea or by lan'?'
  With a hey down and a hey diddle downie.

'No news,' said the beggar, 'no news at a',
  With a hey lillelu and a ho lo lan;
But there is a wedding in the king's ha'.'
  With a hey down and a hey diddle downie.

'Will ye lend me your auld begging weed?
  With a hey lillelu and a ho lo lan;
And I'll give you my riding steed.'
  With a hey down and a hey diddle downie.

'My begging weed will ill suit thee,
  With a hey lillelu and a ho lo lan;
And your riding steed will ill suit me.'
  With a hey down and a hey diddle downie.

'Will you lend me your wig o' hair,
  With a hey lillelu and a ho lo lan;
To cover mine, because it is fair?'
  With a hey down and a hey diddle downie.

But part by right, and part by wrang,
  With a hey lillelu and a ho lo lan;
Frae the beggar man the cloak he wan.
  With a hey down and a hey diddle downie.

The auld beggar man was bound for to ride,
  With a hey lillelu and a ho lo lan;
But young Hynd Horn was bound for the bride.
  With a hey down and a hey diddle downie.

 *weed = clothes.*

When he came to the King's gate,
  With a hey lillelu and a ho lo lan;
He sought a drink for Hynd Horn's sake.
  With a hey down and a hey diddle downie.

The bride came tripping down the stair,
  With a hey lillelu and a ho lo lan;
Wi' the sales o' red gowd in her hair.
  With a hey down and a hey diddle downie.

A cup o' red wine in her hand,
  With a hey lillelu and a ho lo lan;
And that she gae to the auld beggar man.
  With a hey down and a hey diddle downie.

Out o' the cup he drank the wine,
  With a hey lillelu and a ho lo lan;
And into the cup he dropt the ring.
  With a hey down and a hey diddle downie.

'O got ye 't by sea, or got ye 't by land,
  With a hey lillelu and a ho lo lan;
Or got ye 't on a drownd man's hand?'
  With a hey down and a hey diddle downie.

'I got it not by sea, nor got it by land,
  With a hey lillelu and a ho lo lan;
Nor got I it on a drownd man's hand.
  With a hey down and a hey diddle downie.

'But I got it at my wooing gay,
  With a hey lillelu and a ho lo lan;
And I 'll gie 't you on your wedding day.'
  With a hey down and a hey diddle downie.

' O, I 'll cast off my gowns of brown,
With a hey lillelu and a ho lo lan ;
And beg wi' you frae town to town.
With a hey down and a hey diddle downie.

' O, I 'll cast off my gowns of red,
With a hey lillelu and a ho lo lan ;
And I 'll beg wi' you to win my bread.
With a hey down and a hey diddle downie.

' I 'll take the red gowd frae my hair.
With a hey lillelu and a ho lo lan :
And follow you for evermair.'
With a hey down and a hey diddle downie.

' Ye needna cast off your gowns of brown,
With a hey lillelu and a ho lo lan ;
For I 'll make you a lady o' many a town,
With a hey down and a hey diddle downie.

' Ye needna cast off your gowns o' red,
With a hey lillelu and a ho lo lan ;
For it 's only a sham, the begging o' my bread.'
With a hey down and a hey diddle downie.

And atween the kitchen and the ha',
With a hey lillelu and a ho lo lan ;
He loot his cloutie cloak down fa',
With a hey down and a hey diddle downie.

And the red gowd shined ower him a',
With a hey lillelu and a ho lo lan ;
And the bride from the bridegroom was stown awa'.
With a hey down and a hey diddle downie.

 *loot = let.*   *stown = stolen.*

Helen of Kirconnell

I WISH I were where Helen lies,
  Night and day on me she cries,
  O that I were where Helen lies,
On fair Kirconnell Lee!

Curst be the heart that thought the thought,
And curst the hand that fired the shot,
When in my arms burd Helen dropt,
On fair Kirconnell Lee!

O think na ye my heart was sair,
When my love drop't down and spak nae mair!
There did she swoon wi' meikle care,
On fair Kirconnell Lee.

As I went down the water side,
None but my foe to be my guide,
None but my foe to be my guide,
On fair Kirconnell Lee.

I lighted down, my sword did draw,
I hacked him in pieces sma';
I hacked him in pieces sma';
On fair Kirconnell Lee.

O Helen fair, beyond compare,
I 'll make a garland of thy hair,
Shall bund my heart for evermair,
On fair Kirconnell Lee.

O that I were where Helen lies!
Night and day on me she cries,
Out of my bed she bids me rise,
On fair Kirconnell Lee.

O Helen fair, O Helen chaste!
If I were with thee, I were blest,
Where thou lies now, and takes thy rest,
On fair Kirconnell Lee.

I wish my grave were growing green,
A winding sheet drawn ower my e'en,
And I in Helen's arms lying,
On fair Kirconnell Lee.

I wish I were where Helen lies,
Night and day on me she cries,
And I am weary of the skies,
On fair Kirconnell Lee.

The Bailiff's Daughter of Islington

THERE was a youth, and a well-belov'd youth,
　　And he was a squire's son,
　　He loved the bayliff's daughter dear,
That lived in Islington.

But she was coy, and she would not believe
That he did love her so,
No, nor at any time she would
Any countenance to him show.

But when his friends did understand
His fond and foolish mind,
They sent him up to fair London,
An apprentice for to bind.

And when he had been seven long years,
And his love he had not seen,
'Many a tear have I shed for her sake
When she little thought of me.'

All the maids of Islington
Went forth to sport and play;
All but the bayliff's daughter dear;
She secretly stole away.

She put off her gown of gray,
And put on her puggish attire;
She's up to fair London gone,
Her true-love to require.

puggish = ragged.

As she went along the road,
The weather being hot and dry,
There was she aware of her true-love
At length came riding by.

She step't to him, as red as any rose,
And took him by the bridle-ring;
'I pray you, kind sir, give me one penny,
To ease my weary limb.'

'I prithee, sweetheart, canst thou tell me
Where that thou wast born?'
'At Islington, kind sir,' said she,
'Where I have had many a scorn.'

'I prithee, sweetheart, canst thou tell me
Whether thou dost know
The bailiff's daughter of Islington?'
'She's dead, sir, long ago.'

'Then will I sell my goodly steed,
My saddle and my bow;
I will into some far country,
Where no man doth me know.'

'O stay, O stay, thou goodly youth,
She's alive, she is not dead;
Here she standeth by thy side,
And is ready to be thy bride.'

'O farewell grief, and welcome joy,
Ten thousand times and more!
For now I have seen my own true-love,
That I thought I should have seen no more.'

Rare Willie drowned in Yarrow

'WILLY 'S rare, and Willy 's fair,
    And Willy 's wondrous bonny;
    And Willy heght to marry me,
Gin e'er he marry'd ony.

Yestreen I made my bed fu' braid,
The night I 'll make it narrow,
For a' the live-long winter's night
I lie twin'd of my marrow.

O came you by yon water-side?
Pu'd you the rose or lilly?
Or came you by yon meadow green?
Or saw you my sweet Willy?

She sought him east, she sought him west,
She sought him brade and narrow;
Sine, in the clifting of a craig,
She found him drown'd in Yarrow.

 *heght* = promised.   *marrow* = mate.   *clifting* = cleft.

The Gypsy Laddie

THERE come seven gypsies on a day,
  Oh, but they sang bonny, O!
And they sang so sweet, and they sang so clear,
Down cam the earl's ladie, O.

O she came tripping down the stair,
  Wi' a' her maids afore her;
As soon as they saw her weel-fared face,
  They cast their glamoury o'er her.

They gave to her the nutmeg,
  And they gave to her the ginger;
But she gave to them a far better thing,
  The seven gold rings off her fingers.

When the earl he did come home,
  Inquiring for his ladie,
One of the servants made this reply,
  'She 's awa' with the gypsie laddie.'

'Come saddle for me the brown,' he said,
  'For the black was ne'er so speedy,
And I will travel night and day
  Till I find out my ladie.

'Will you come home, my dear?' he said,
  Oh, will you come home, my honey?
And, by the point of my broad sword,
  A hand I 'll ne'er lay on you.'

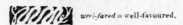 weel-fared = well-favoured.

THE GYPSY LADDIE

' Last night I lay on a good feather-bed,
   And my own wedded lord beside me,
And to-night I 'll lie in the ash-corner,
   With the gypsies all around me.

' They took off my high-heeled shoes,
   That were made of Spanish leather,
And I have put on coars Lowland brogues,
   To trip it o'er the heather.'

The Earl of Cashan is lying sick ;
   Not one hair I 'm sorry ;
I 'd rather have a kiss from his fair lady's lips
   Than all his gold and his money.

Clyde Water

WILLIE stands in his stable door,
  And clapping at his steed
  And looking o'er his white fingers
His nose began to bleed.

'Gie corn unto my horse, mother,
Gie meat unto my man,
For I maun gang to Maggie's bower
Before the nicht comes on.'

'O bide this night wi' me, Willie,
O bide this night wi' me;
The bestan' cock o' a' the roost
At your supper shall be.'

'A' your cocks, and a' your roosts,
I value not a prin,
For I 'll awa' to Maggie's bower;
I 'll win ere she lie down.'

'Stay this night wi' me, Willie,
O stay this night wi' me;
The bestan' sheep in a' the flock
At your supper shall be.'

'A' your sheep, and a' your flocks,
I value not a prin,
For I 'll awa' to Maggie's bower;
I 'll win ere she lie down.'

 prin = pin.

'O an' ye gang to Maggie's bower,
Sae sair against my will,
The deepest pot in Clyde's water,
My malison ye 's feel.'

'The guid steed that I ride upon
Cost me thrice thretty pound;
And I 'll put trust in his swift feet,
To hae me safe to land.'

As he rade ower yon high, high hill,
And down yon dowie den,
The noise that was in Clyde's water
Wou'd fear'd five hun'er men.

'O roaring Clyde, ye roar ower loud,
Your streams seem wondrous strang;
Make me your wreck as I come back,
But spare me as I gang.'

Then he is on to Maggie's bower,
And tirled at the pin;
'O sleep ye, wake ye, Maggie,' he said,
'Ye 'll open, lat me come in.'

'O wha is this at my bower-door,
That calls me by my name?'
'It is your first love, sweet Willie,
This night newly come hame.

'O open the door to me, Maggie,
O open and let me in;
My boots are fu' o' Clyde's water,
I 'm shivering at the chin.'

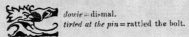

dowie = dismal.
tirled at the pin = rattled the bolt.

'I darena open the door to you,
Nor darena lat you in;
For my mither she is fast asleep
An' I darena mak' nae din.'

'O gin ye winna open the door,
Nor yet be kind to me,
Now tell me o' some out-chamber,
Where I this nicht may be.'

'My barns are fu' o' corn, Willie,
My stables are fu' o' hay;
My bowers are fu' o' gentlemen,
They 'll nae remove till day ! '

'O fare ye well, my fause Maggie,
O farewell, and adieu !
I 've gotten my mither's malison
This night coming to you.'

As he rode ower yon high, high hill,
And down yon dowie den,
The rushing that was in Clyde's water
Took Willie's cane frae him.

He lean'd him ower his saddle-bow,
To catch his cane again ;
The rushing that was in Clyde's water
Took Willie's hat frae him.

He lean'd him ower his saddle-bow,
To catch his hat thro' force ;
The rushing that was in Clyde's water
Took Willie frae his horse.

' How can I turn to my horse head
And learn how to sowm ?
I 've gotten my mither's malison,
It 's here that I maun drown.'

The very hour this young man sank,
Into the pot sae deep,
Up it wakened his love, Maggie,
Out o' her drowsy sleep.

' Come here, come here, my mither, dear,
And read this dreary dream ;
I dream'd my love was at our gates,
And nane wad let him in.'

' Lye still, lye still, now, my Maggie,
Lye still and tak your rest ;
Sin' your true-love was at your gates,
It 's but twa quarters past.'

Nimbly, nimbly, raise she up
And nimbly pat she on,
And the higher that the lady cried,
The louder blew the win'.

The firstan' step that she stepp'd in,
She stepped to the queet ;
' Ohon, alas ! ' said that lady,
' This water 's wondrous deep.'

The nextan' step that she wade in,
She waded to the knee ;
Says she, ' I cou'd wade farther in,
If I my love cou'd see.'

sowm = swim.
queet = ankle.

K

The nextan' step that she wade in,
She waded to the chin ;
The deepest pot in Clyde's water
She got sweet Willie in.

' You 've had a cruel mither, Willie,
And I have had anither,
But we shall sleep in Clyde's water
Like sister an' like brither.'

The Lady turned Serving-Man

YOU beautious ladies, great and small,
   I write unto you one and all,
      Whereby that you may understand,
What I have suffered in this land.

I was by birth a lady fair,
My father's chief and onely heir,
But when my good old father dy'd,
Then was I made a young knight's bride.

And then my love built me a bower
Bedeck't with many a fragrant flower;
A braver bower you never did see
Then my true-love did build for me.

But there came thieves late in the night,
They rob'd my bower, and slew my knight.
And after that my knight was slain,
I could no longer there remain.

My servants all from me did flye,
In the midst of my extremity,
And left me by myself alone,
With a heart more cold than any stone.

Yet, though my heart was full of care,
Heaven would not suffer me to despair,
Wherefore in hast I chang'd my name,
From Fair Elsie to Sweet William.

And therewithal I cut my hair,
And drest myself in man's attire,
My doublet, hose, and bever-hat,
And a golden band about my neck.

With a silver rapier by my side,
So like a gallant I did ride,
The thing that I delighted on,
Was for to be a serving-man.

Thus in my sumptuous man's array,
I bravely rode along the way,
And at the last it chanced it so
That I unto the king's court did go.

Then to the king I bowed full low,
My love and duty for to show,
And so much favour I did crave,
That I a serving-man's place might have.

'Stand up, brave youth,' the king reply'd,
'Thy service shall not be deny'd;
But tell me first what thou canst do;
Thou shalt be fitted thereunto.

'Wilt thou be usher of my hall,
To wait upon my nobles all?
Or wilt thou be taster of my wine,
To wait on me when I shall dine?

'Or wilt thou be my chamberlain,
To make my bed both soft and fine?
Or wilt thou be one of my guard,
And I will give thee thy reward.'

Sweet William, with a smiling face,
Said to the king, 'If 't please your grace,
To show such favour unto me,
Your chamberlain I fain would be.'

The king then did the nobles call,
To ask the counsel of them all,
Who gave consent Sweet William he
The king's own chamberlain should be.

Now mark what strange things came to pass:
As the king one day a hunting was,
With all his lords and noble train,
Sweet William did at home remain.

Sweet William had no company then
With him at home but an old man,
And when he saw the coast was clear,
He took a lute which he had there.

Upon the lute sweet William plaid,
And to the same he sung and said,
With a pleasant and most noble voice,
Which made the old man to rejoyce:

'My father was as brave a lord
As ever Europe did afford;
My mother was a lady bright,
My husband was a valiant knight.

'And I myself a lady gay
Bedeck't with gorgeous, rich array;
The bravest lady in the land
Had not more pleasures to command.

'I had my musick every day,
Harmonious lessons for to play,
I had my virgins fair and free
Continually to wait on me.

'But now, alas! my husband's dead,
And all my friends are from me fled,
My former joys are past and gone,
For now I am a serving-man.'

At last the king from hunting came,
And presently upon the same
He call'd for the good old man,
And thus to speak the king began.

'What news, what news, old man,' quod he;
'What news hast thou to tell to me?'
'Brave news,' the old man he did say,
'Sweet William is a lady gay.'

' If this be true thou tellest me,
I 'le make thee a lord of high degree ;
But if thy words do prove a lye,
Thou shalt be hanged up presently.'

But when the king the truth had found,
His joys did more and more abound ;
According as the old man did say,
Sweet William was a lady gay.

Therefore the king without delay
Put on her glorious rich array,
And upon her head a crown of gold,
Which was most famous to behold.

And then, for fear of further strife,
He took Sweet William for his wife ;
The like before was never seen,
A serving-man to be a queen.

OLD·CARL·HOOD :
HE'S AYE·FOR·ILL·AND·NEVER·FOR·GOOD

Earl Brand

OH did ye ever hear o' brave Earl Brand?
    Ay lally, o lilly lally;
    He courted the king's daughter of fair England,
  All i' the night sae early.

She was scarcely fifteen years of age,
    Ay lally, o lilly lally;
Till sae boldly she came to his bedside,
    All i' the night sae early.

'O Earl Bran', fain wad I see,
    Ay lally, o lilly lally;
A pack of hounds let loose on the lea,'
    All i' the night sae early.

'O lady, I have no steeds but one,
  Ay lally, o lilly lally;
And thou shalt ride, and I will run,'
  All i' the night sae early.

'O Earl Bran', my father has two,
  Ay lally, o lilly lally;
And thou shall have the best o' them a','
  All i' the night sae early.

They have ridden o'er moss and moor,
  Ay lally, o lilly lally;
And they met neither rich nor poor,
  All i' the night sae early.

Until they met with old Carl Hood;
  Ay lally, o lilly lally;
He 's aye for ill, and never for good,
  All i' the night sae early.

'Earl Bran', if ye love me,
  Aye lally, o lilly lally;
Seize this old carl, and gar him die,'
  All i' the night sae early.

'O lady fair, it wad be sair,
  Ay lally, o lilly lally;
To slay an old man that has grey hair.
  All i' the night sae early.

'O lady fair, I 'll no do sae;
  Ay lally, o lilly lally;
I 'll gie him a pound, and let him gae,'
  All i' the night sae early.

gar – cause.

'O where hae ye ridden this lee lang day?
  Ay lally, o lilly lally;
Or where hae ye stolen this lady away?'
  All i' the night sae early.

'I have not ridden this lee lang day,
  Ay lally, o lilly lally;
Nor yet have I stolen this lady away,
  All i' the night sae early.

'She is my only, my sick sister,
  Ay lally, o lilly lally;
Whom I have brought from Winchester,'
  All i' the night sae early.

'If she be sick, and like to dead,
  Ay lally, o lilly lally;
Why wears she the ribbon sae red?
  All i' the night sae early.

'If she be sick, and like to die,
  Ay lally, o lilly lally;
Then why wears she the gold on high?'
  All i' the night sae early.

When he came to this lady's gate,
  Ay lally, o lilly lally;
Sae rudely as he rapped at it,
  All i' the night sae early.

'O where's the lady o' this ha'?'
  Ay lally, o lilly lally;
'She's out with her maids to play at the ba','
  All i' the night sae early.

'Ha, ha, ha! ye are a' mista'en:
  Ay lally, o lilly lally;
Gae count your maidens o'er again,
  All i' the night sae early.

'I saw her far beyond the lea,
  Ay lally, o lilly lally;
Away the Earl Bran's lover to be,'
  All i' the night sae early.

The father armed fifteen of his best men,
  Ay lally, o lilly lally;
To bring his daughter back again,
  All i' the night sae early.

O'er her left shoulder the lady looked then:
  Ay lally, o lilly lally;
'O Earl Bran', we both are ta'en,'
  All i' the night sae early.

'If they come on me ane by ane,
  Ay lally, o lilly lally;
Ye may stand by and see them slain,
  All i' the night sae early.

'But if they come on me one and all,
  Ay lally, o lilly lally;
Ye may stand by and see me fall,'
  All i' the night sae early.

They have come on him ane by ane,
  Ay lally, o lilly lally;
And he has killed them all but ane,
  All i' the night sae early.

And that ane came behind his back,
  Ay lally, o lilly lally;
And he 's gien him a deadly whack,
  All i' the night sae early.

But for a' sae wounded as Earl Bran' was,
  Ay lally, o lilly lally;
He has set his lady on her horse,
  All i' the night sae early.

They rode till they came to the water o' Doune,
  Ay lally, o lilly lally;
And then he alighted to wash his wounds,
  All i' the night sae early.

'O Earl Bran', I see your heart's blood!'
  Ay lally, o lilly lally;
''Tis but the gleat o' my scarlet hood,'
  All i' the night sae early.

They rode till they came to his mother's gate,
  Ay lally, o lilly lally;
And sae rudely as he rapped at it,
  All i' the night sae early.

'O my son 's slain, my son 's put down,
  Ay lally, o lilly lally;
And a' for the sake of an English loun,'
  All i' the night sae early.

'O say not sae, my dear mother,
  Ay lally, o lilly lally;
But marry her to my youngest brother,
  All i' the night sae early.

'This has not been the death o' ane,
  Ay lally, o lilly lally;
But it 's been that of fair seventeen,'
  All i' the night sae early.

Earl Richard

'O LADY, rock never your young son young,
  One hour langer for me;
    For I have a sweetheart in Garlioch Wells,
I love far better than thee.

'The very sole o' that lady's foot
  Than thy face is far mair white';
'But nevertheless, now, Erl Richard,
  Ye will bide in my bower a' night.'

She birled him with the ale and wine,
  As they sat down to sup:
A living man he laid him down,
  But I wot he ne'er rose up.

 *birled* = plied.

Then up and spake the popinjay,
   That flew aboun her head ;
‘ Lady ! keep weel your green cleiding
   Frae gude Erl Richard’s bleid.’

‘ O better I ’ll keep my green cleiding
   Frae gude Erl Richard’s bleid,
Than thou canst keep thy clattering toung,
   That trattles in thy head.’

She has call’d upon her bower maidens,
   She has call’d them ane by ane ;
‘ There lies a dead man in my bour :
   I wish that he were gane ! ’

They hae booted him, and spurred him,
   As he was wont to ride ;
A hunting-horn tied round his waist,
   A sharpe sword by his side ;
And they hae had him to the wan water,
   For a’ men call it Clyde.

Then up and spoke the popinjay,
   That sat upon the tree—
‘ What hae ye done wi’ Erl Richard ?
   Ye were his gay ladye.’

‘ Come down, come down, my bonny bird,
   And sit upon my hand ;
And thou sall hae a cage o’ gowd,
   Where thou hast but a wand.’

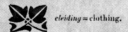 *cleiding* = clothing.

'Awa! awa! ye ill woman;
  Nae cage o' gowd for me;
As ye hae dune to Erl Richard,
  Sae wad ye do to me.'

She hadna cross'd a rigg o' land,
  A rigg, but barely ane,
When she met wi' his auld father,
  Came riding all alane.

'Where hae ye been, now, ladye fair,
  Where hae ye been sae late?'
'We hae been seeking Erl Richard,
  But him we canna get.'

'Erl Richard kens a' the fords in Clyde,
  He'll ride them ane by ane;
And though the night was ne'er sae mirk,
  Erl Richard will be hame.'

The ladye turned her round about,
  Wi' meikle mournin' din—
'I fears me sair o' Clyde water,
  That he is drown'd therein.'

O it fell ance upon a day,
  The king was boun' to ride;
And he has mist him, Erl Richard
  Should hae ridden on his right side.

'Gar douk, gar douk,' the king he cried,
  'Gar douk for gold and fee;
O wha will douk for Erl Richard's sake,
  Or wha will douk for me?'

rigg = ridge
douk = dive.

They douked in at ae weil-head,
   And out ay at the other;
' We can douk nae mair for Erl Richard,
   Although he were our brother.'

It fell that, in that ladye's castle,
   The king was boun' to bed;
And up and spake the popinjay,
   That flew abune his head.

' Leave off your douking on the day,
   And douk upon the night;
And where that sackless knight lies slain,
   The candles will burn bright.'

' O there 's a bird within this bower,
   That sings baith sad and sweet;
O there 's a bird within your bower,
   Keeps me frae my night's sleep.'

They left the douking on the day,
   And douked upon the night;
And, where that sackless knight lay slain,
   The candles burned bright.

The deepest pot in a' the linn,
   They fand Erl Richard in;
A grene turf tyed across his breast,
   To keep that gude lord down.

Then up and spake the king himsell,
   When he saw the deadly wound—
' O wha has slain my right-hand man,
   That held my hawk and hound ? '

weil-head = eddy.   *sackless* = guiltless.
linn = stream.

L

Then up and spake the popinjay,
  Says—'What needs a' this din?
It was his gay lady took his life,
  And hided him in the linn.'

She swore her by the grass sae grene,
  Sae did she by the corn,
She hadna seen him, Erl Richard,
  Since Moninday at morn.

'Put na the wite on me,' she said;
  'It was my may Catherine.'
Then they hae cut baith fern and thorn,
  To burn that maiden in.

It wadna take upon her cheik,
  Nor yet upon her chin;
Nor yet upon her yellow hair,
  To cleanse the deadly sin.

The maiden touched the clay-cauld corpse,
  A drap it never bled;
The ladye laid her hand on him,
  And soon the ground was red.

Out they hae ta'en her, may Catherine,
  And put her mistress in:
The flame tuik fast upon her cheik,
  Tuik fast upon her chin;
Tuik fast upon her faire bodye—
  She burn'd like hollins green.

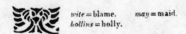

wite = blame.   *may* = maid.
hollins = holly.

The Fair Flower of Northumberland

IT was a knight in Scotland borne,
   Follow, my love, come over the strand,
   Was taken prisoner, and left forlorne,
Even by the good Earle of Northumberland.

Then was he cast in prison strong,
Follow, my love, come over the strand,
Where he could not walke nor lie along,
Even by the good Earle of Northumberland.

And as in sorrow thus he lay,
Follow, my love, come over the strand,
The Earle's sweet daughter walked that way,
And she was the faire flower of Northumberland.

And passing by, like an angel bright,
Follow, my love, come over the strand,
The prisoner had of her a sight,
And she the faire flower of Northumberland.

And loud to her this knight did crie,
Follow, my love, come over the strand,
The salt teares standing in his eye,
And she the faire flower of Northumberland.

'Faire lady,' he said, 'take pity on me,
Follow, my love, come over the strand,
And let me not in prison dye,
And you the faire flower of Northumberland.'

'Faire Sir, how should I take pity on thee,
Follow, my love, come over the strand.
Thou being a foe to our countrie,
And I the faire flower of Northumberland?'

'Faire lady, I am no foe,' he said,
Follow, my love, come over the strand.
'Through thy sweet love heere was I stay'd,
For thee, the faire flower of Northumberland.'

'Why shouldst thou come heere for love of me,
Follow, my love, come over the strand,
Having wife and children in thy countrie?
And I the faire flower of Northumberland.'

'I sweare by the blessed Trinitie,
Follow, my love, come over the strand,
I have no wife nor children, I
Nor dwelling at home in merrie Scotland.

'If curteously you will set me free,
Follow, my love, come over the strand,
I vow that I will marrie thee,
So soone as I come in faire Scotland.

'Thou shalt be a lady of castles and towers,
Follow, my love, come over the strand,
And sit like a queene in princely bowers.
When I am at home in faire Scotland.'

Then parted hence this lady gay,
Follow, my love, come over the strand,
And got her father's ring away,
To helpe this sad knight into faire Scotland.

Likewise much gold she got by sleight,
Follow, my love, come over the strand,
And all to helpe this forlorne knight,
To wend from her father to faire Scotland.

Two gallant steeds, both good and able,
Follow, my love, come over the strand,
She likewise tooke out of the stable,
To ride with this knight into faire Scotland.

And to the jaylor she sent this ring,
Follow, my love, come over the strand,
The knight from prison forth to bring,
To wend with her into faire Scotland.

This token set the prisoner free,
Follow, my love, come over the strand,
Who straight went to this faire lady,
To wend with her into faire Scotland.

A gallant steede he did bestride,
Follow, my love, come over the strand,
And with the lady away did ride,
And she the faire flower of Northumberland.

They rode till they came to a water cleare,
Follow, my love, come over the strand,
' Good Sir, how should I follow you heere,
And I the faire flower of Northumberland ?

' The water is rough and wonderfull deepe,
Follow, my love, come over the strand,
And on my saddle I shall not keepe,
And I the faire flower of Northumberland.'

L 2

'Feare not the foord, faire lady,' quoth he,
Follow, my love, come over the strand,
'For long I cannot stay with thee,
And thou the faire flower of Northumberland.'

The lady prickt her wanton steed,
Follow, my love, come over the strand,
And over the river swom with speede,
And she the faire flower of Northumberland.

From top to toe all wet was shee,
Follow, my love, come over the strand,
'This have I done for love of thee,
And I the faire flower of Northumberland.'

Thus rode she all one winter's night,
Follow, my love, come over the strand,
Till Edenborow they saw in sight,
The chiefest towne in all Scotland.

Quoth he, 'I have wife, and children five,
Follow, my love, come over the strand,
In Edenborow they be alive;
Then get thee home to faire England.

'This favour shalt thou have to boote,
Follow, my love, come over the strand,
Ile have thy horse, go thou on foote,
Go, get thee home to Northumberland.'

'O false and faithless knight,' quoth shee,
Follow, my love, come over the strand,
'And canst thou deale so bad with me,
And I the faire flower of Northumberland?

' Dishonour not a ladie's name,
Follow, my love, come over the strand,
But draw thy sword and end my shame,
And I the faire flower of Northumberland.'

He tooke her from her stately steed,
Follow, my love, come over the strand,
And left her there in extreme need,
And she the faire flower of Northumberland.

Then sate she down full heavily ;
Follow, my love, come over the strand,
At length two knights came riding by,
Two gallant knights of faire England.

She fell down humbly on her knee,
Follow, my love, come over the strand,
Saying, ' Courteous knights, take pittie on me,
And I the faire flower of Northumberland.

' I have offended my father deere,
Follow, my love, come over the strand,
And by a false knight that brought me heere,
From the good Earle of Northumberland.'

They tooke her up behind them then,
Follow, my love, come over the strand,
And brought her to her father's againe,
And he the good Earle of Northumberland.

All you faire maidens be warned by me,
Follow, my love, come over the strand,
Scots were never true, nor never will be,
To lord, nor lady, nor faire England.

THE·WIFE·OF
USHER'S·WELL

THERE lived a wife at Usher's Well,
    And a wealthy wife was she;
      She had three stout and stalwart sons,
And sent them o'er the sea.

They hadna been a week from her,
A week but barely ane,
Whan word came to the carline wife,
That her three sons were gane.

They hadna been a week from her,
A week but barely three,
Whan word came to the carline wife,
That her sons she 'd never see.

 *carline* = old woman.

'I wish the wind may never cease,
Nor fashes in the flood,
Till my three sons come hame to me,
In earthly flesh and blood.'

It fell about the Martinmas,
Whan nights are lang and mirk,
The carline wife's three sons came hame,
And their hats were o' the birk.

It neither grew in syke nor ditch,
Nor yet in ony sheugh,
But at the gates o' Paradise,
That birk grew fair eneugh.

'Blow up the fire, my maidens!
Bring water from the well!
For a' my house shall feast this night,
Since my three sons are well.'

And she has made to them a bed,
She 's made it large and wide;
And she 's ta'en her mantle her about,
Sat down at the bedside.

Up then crew the red, red cock,
And up and crew the gray;
The eldest to the youngest said,
' 'Tis time we were away.'

The cock he hadna craw'd but once,
And clapp'd his wings at a',
Whan the youngest to the eldest said,
'Brother, we must awa'.

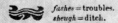 *fashes* = troubles.   *syke* = marshy hollow.
sheugh = ditch.

'The cock doth craw, the day doth daw,
The channerin' worm doth chide;
Gin we be missed out o' our place,
A sair pain we maun bide.

'Fare ye weel, my mother dear!
Fareweel to barn and byre,
And fare ye weel, the bonny lass,
That kindles my mother's fire.'

channerin' = fretting.